READY, SET, CHANGE!

Advance Praise for

READY, SET, CHANGE!

"In conventional management thought, the people are seen correctly as being resistant to change. Embracing this accurate assumption leads the manager to initiate change efforts that can only fail. The paradox is resolved when one learns what it means to create change readiness in inherently fearful human beings. If you internalize what is in this book, you will become what organizations need but cannot obtain, an effective leader of change."

— Professor Robert E. Quinn, Co-author of *The Economics of Higher Purpose: Eight Counter Intuitive Steps for Creating a Purpose Driven Organization*

"Ready, set, story time! April has broken the traditional prescriptive business book model by using storytelling to package complex elements of change management into easy to understand insights. It's a refreshing way to absorb valuable tools and initiatives for implementing change in the workplace."

"Change is hard, but it doesn't have to be complicated. April Callis-Birchmeier outlines how to set yourself to lead large-scale change by getting your people ready and by giving them a clear picture of where you're headed. This book will make your organizational change a little easier, and more likely to succeed."

"I've personally worked with April on a major change management initiative at a large healthcare system. No one brings a more innovative, easy-to-use approach for moving organizations forward! This book is your guide to making change painless in your career and your organization."

READY, SET, CHANGE!

Simplify and Accelerate
Organizational Change

April Callis-Birchmeier, CCMP™, PMP

Printed in the United States of America

First Printing, 2020

ISBN: 978-0-9765171-3-9

Ordering Information:
Quantity sales. Special discounts are available on quantity purchases by corporations, associations, and others who purchase directly from the publisher. Contact april@springboard-consult.com for details.

For my husband, Jay, thank you for your love and belief.

And to my parents, John and Carol, for everything.

Table of Contents

Foreword

by Dave Ulrich

*Rensis Likert Professor, Ross School of Business,
University of Michigan Partner, The RBL Group*

A number of years ago, a prominent business school hosted a conference and invited me to participate in workshop for individuals who had been prominent in shaping how organizations "managed change." The ambitious goal of this event was to find a definitive and integrated approach to better make change happen.

I refused to their kind invitation to this conference. The intent of a single unifying change model was kind of like trying to make Esperanto the universal language to unite the world. There have been, are, and likely will continue to be numerous languages that reflect cultural heritages and national differences.

Likewise, there are many approaches of how to "make change happen" that have been proposed. (See *Table 1* for some prominent examples of proposed change processes.)

Even with these many models from thoughtful colleagues, the demands of change (lately called agility, flexibility, transformation, disruption) continue. Few doubt that the business context (social, technology, economic, political, environmental, and demographic) is dramatically changing (see future of work 2.0, 3.0, 4.0 ... 99.0!). Without doubt, individuals and organization have to anticipate and adapt to change or get left behind.

Popular Change Processes				
Author	Warner Burke	John Kotter	Dale Lake	Price Pritchett
Example work	*Organization Change*	*Leading Change*	*Change Manual*	*Quantum Leap*
Change processes	• Be self-aware • Monitor external environment • Establish a need for change • Provide clear vision or direction • Communicate the need • Deal with resistance • Leverage multiple actions • Have consistency and persistence	• Establish sense of urgency • Create guiding coalition • Develop vision or strategy • Communication change vision • Empower employees for action • Generate short term wins • Consolidate gains and produce more change • Anchor new approaches in culture	• Design a change agenda • Assess the current situation • Create dis-satisfaction or need for change • Activate change champions • Influence stakeholders • Assess and overcome resistance • Build team and network • Structure for success • Do project management • Monitor progress • Have continuous learning	• Give clear marching orders • Nail down each job • Manage resistance to change • Encourage risk taking • Create supportive work environment • Attend to transition and change • Take care of "me" issues • Communicate over and over again

Table 1: Popular Change Processes

Popular Change Processes				
Michael Beer	Hay Group	GE Change Acceleration process	Sean Covey	Ed Lawler and Chris Worley
Organization Change and Development	*This is the Hay Model for Change*	*Change Acceleration Process*	*Disciplines of Execution*	*The Agility Factor*
• Dissatisfaction • Model or purpose of change • Success or outcomes • Cost of change • Resistance to change	• Ensure reasons for change • Identify "change agents" • Assess stakeholders and sponsors • Plan project activities • Communicate changes • Assess impact on people and structure • Address the impacts of the change. • Share process change. • Support changes • Train for new skills • Measure and report on progress	• Lead change • Create a felt need • Define a direction or shape a vision • Mobilize commitment • Make decisions • Dedicate resources • Learn, adapt, monitor	• Focus • Empowerment • Leverage • Accountability	• Strategizing dynamically • Perceiving environmental change • Testing responses • Implementing change • Accountability

Table 1: Popular Change Processes

Helping people and organizations change is an increasing challenge and opportunity. The challenge is not knowing just what to do, but how to really do it. My mentor and colleague Steve Kerr taught me a remarkably simple but insightful formula: $Q = E * A$. Q is quality of the activity (in this case the ability to make change happen). E is the effectiveness of the approach (in this case the processes to be used like those in Table 1). A is the acceptance and use of the process. Steve (and others, including me) argue that in the change literature we have many good "E" (effective processes for making change happen), but we have too few "A" (acceptance and use of the processes). High E (e.g., 9 out of 10) to improve quality of change without high A (e.g., 2 out of 10) will fail ($9 * 2 = 18$ out of a possible 100 score). So, the opportunity of improving organization and people's ability to change requires not just another model of what to do (high E), but a commitment to actually do it (high A).

This is where this outstanding book by April Callis-Birchmeier adds enormous value. She proposes a very thoughtful 5-step process for making change happen:

R	Relevant and relatable messaging about the change
E	Engage Leaders as sponsors and actively promote the change
A	Advance communication to ensure messaging is received and advocating for stakeholders
D	Develop support and train on process and technology
Y	Reinforce WHY and reduce resistance to adoption

These are five outstanding steps for change. They could be easily added to other thought leaders in Table 1. They are high "E" (effective list of what makes change work).

But, what makes April's work in this book really unique and powerful is how she builds the "A" (acceptance of change).

First, she focuses on both individuals and organizations. Her five basic principles (READY) apply to both individuals facing change (e.g. personal habit improvement) and organizations responding to change business conditions (e.g., new strategic agenda). Her 5 basic change principles apply to across settings.

Second, while she confirms other change processes, her real value added is making these processes come alive and real. We are introduced to Elizabeth (HR), Jake (friend and project manager), and Allie (consultant). We experience with them the application of these READY change principles to personal goals (e.g., running) and organizational improvements.

Third, her work is less about a fundamentally new and universal "theory of change" and more a pragmatic and useful approach to doing change: *My goal of including a narrative in this book was to show how concepts are put into action and to recognize that readiness can apply to personal events as well as impact our professional lives.*

She accomplishes her goal with ideas, stories, and tools that increase the "A" (acceptance of change).

I am delighted to reinforce April's personal desire to improve the **Quality** of change efforts by maintaining highly **Effective** ideas, but really allowing those ideas to have high **Acceptance**!

Kudos for a marvelous book.

Dave Ulrich
Alpine Utah
February 2020

Introduction

On the bright, sunny morning of October 1, 2013, a high-stakes, high-visibility technology disaster began to unfold with the launch of the HealthCare.gov system. The Affordable Care Act (ACA), passed in 2010, was the crowning achievement of the Obama Administration. The ACA required a federal website to facilitate the purchase of private health insurance for people living in states without established health insurance marketplaces.

On that Tuesday morning, and for weeks after, HealthCare.gov users were met with website outages and technical malfunctions. By mid-October, just a handful of the 14.6 million people who visited the federal exchange website had managed to enroll in insurance plans. Of the enrollments that were accepted, many were marred by mistakes. Because so many insurance companies have similar and confusing names, enrollments were sent to the wrong insurers, sometimes in different states. The loss of crucial information made enrollment files unusable.

A New York Times researcher, for example, managed to register at 6 a.m. on October 1. Despite more than forty attempts over the next eleven days, she was never able to log in. Her attempts, like those of many other Americans, led to a blank screen.

In hindsight, the disaster was inevitable. A mere four and a half days before the launch of HealthCare.gov, the leadership team of the Centers for Medicare & Medicaid Services (CMS) was worried.

CMS leaders were so concerned about the new system that they visited the primary technology vendor to assess readiness for the system launch.

What they found was alarming.

After limited performance testing it was clear the system couldn't support the anticipated demands of concurrent users of HealthCare.gov. CMS officials requested that the computing infrastructure contractor double the capacity within 72 hours. The contractor "pulled gear from all over the world, renting planes to get hardware here that was intended for other clients."[1]

On its opening day, HealthCare.gov experienced 250,000 concurrent users. Website outages began within two hours of launch, preventing many consumers from logging in and signing up for health insurance. In the end, only six consumers successfully registered for mandated coverage on HealthCare.gov's first day.

Technical issues were not the only problem in the implementation of Healthcare.gov. For example, poor marketing and communication

---

1 Levinson, Daniel R. "HealthCare.gov: Case Study of CMS Management of the Federal Marketplace." HealthCare.gov: Case Study of CMS Management of the Federal Marketplace (OEI-06-14-00350) 02-22-2016, HHS Office of the Inspector General, 22 Feb. 2016, oig.hhs.gov/oei/reports/oei-06-14-00350.asp.

meant that 62 percent of Americans were unaware of the October 1 launch date.[2]

The problems at launch created a firestorm of negative publicity and media attention about the system. The website problems were front-page news and created substantial debate among stakeholders, resulting in ten congressional hearings before the end of November.

The process change, communication, sponsorship, training and go-live support for the project was ineffective. The project had many issues which could have been avoided, including:

◊ Lack of clarity and message about why HealthCare.gov mattered to individuals.
◊ Poor leadership engagement and alignment
◊ Organizational culture clashes
◊ Resistance to process simplification
◊ Integration issues between policy and technology
◊ Lack of communication to stakeholders and end users
◊ Poor learning and ongoing support planning

Also on October 1, 2013, I showed up for my first day as a contractor on the Michigan state exchange for the Affordable Care Act (ACA). I'd been hired to lead the Organizational Change Management effort for the Michigan ACA, which at the time was called Medicaid Expansion.

---

2 The Henry J. Kaiser Family Foundation, State Decisions on Health Insurance Marketplaces and the Medicaid Expansion, December 17, 2015. Accessed at http://kff.org/health-reform/state-indicator/state-decisions-for-creating-health-insurance-exchanges-and-expanding-medicaid/ on January 6, 2016.

For me, the first order of business was to work with our marketing and communications area to rename the project from the boring "Michigan Medicaid Expansion" to a friendlier, more relatable name, the Healthy Michigan Plan.

Due to some foot-dragging by the legislature, our implementation date was scheduled for April 1, 2014. (Yes, April Fool's Day!) The technical teams were already working on the state system, which would tie in to the federal HealthCare.gov site. I watched the federal rollout with both great interest and a sense of dread.

With only six months to implement, it was essential to work in tandem with the technical team and policy experts to develop the processes, information and materials to share with citizens in the State of Michigan. Our goal was to enroll 322,000 low-income adults, 19 to 64 years old, in the Healthy Michigan Plan (HMP) by the end of 2014. Our rollout was so successful, however, that we surpassed that number in the first one hundred days!

In the *New England Journal of Medicine* article entitled "Launching the Healthy Michigan Plan – The First 100 Days," author John Z. Ayanian, M.D., identifies several factors which contributed to our successful launch. Among the key factors was the coordination across the policy, technical, and project teams, along with "the methods of outreach to potential enrollees and new communication tools for external groups involved in enrollment."[3]

As a part of the change management approach, we used checklists, "laying out clear goals and deadlines, the checklist facilitated the transparent flow of information between internal and external stakeholders". We also created a communication subgroup with representation from policy, enrollment, technical, project, and change management teams.

Dr. Ayanian also noted our internal website and information toolkit as success factors:

"A toolkit of brochures, advertisements, and social media posts about the program was distributed broadly through existing networks of organizations already working in local communities to drive outreach and enrollment, including the state's primary care and hospital associations, local public health departments, and a broad array of community groups. Given the widely polarized public opinions about the ACA in Michigan and many other states, items in this toolkit described the Healthy Michigan Plan to potential enrollees

---

[3] Ayanian, John Z., et al. "Launching the Healthy Michigan Plan - The First 100 Days: NEJM." *New England Journal of Medicine*, New England Journal of Medicine, 23 Oct. 2014, www.nejm.org/doi/full/10.1056/NEJMp1409600.

as a state initiative for working-age adults rather than as a component of the ACA."[4]

The success of the Healthy Michigan Plan has been acknowledged in articles, white papers, and case studies. The rollout of the HealthCare.gov site and the Healthy Michigan Plan couldn't have been more different. The difference? Our team used Organizational Change Management to prepare users and stakeholders.

In this world of nearly constant change, I'm often asked how best to help people adopt new technology. This is a question without a complete answer. Because individuals make up organizations, and organizations rely on individuals to adopt and sustain change, there is no one answer to the question. Readiness is more than training. You can prepare and practice, but readiness is an emotional and mental choice It's a decision that's made either knowingly or unknowingly, and one which can have a lasting impact by directing our course of action.

As an Organizational Change Management expert and consultant who advises organizations on how to improve success of their change efforts, my goal is to share what I've learned through experience, expertise and my observation of implementation outcomes. Human Resource professionals, project managers and change practitioners are often assigned to assist on technology projects and change initiatives without the benefit of a simple framework to help users get ready for change. This book is written for those who lead change – with or

---

[4]   Michigan.gov. *Healthy Michigan Plan Toolkit.* August 5, 2014. http://www.michigan.gov/healthymiplan/0,5668,7-326--325186--,00.html.

without experience – and provides an easy-to-follow approach. I've created this guide with both a business fable and a specific framework to guide you through the journey of change.

The fable narrative features Elizabeth, a Human Resource Manager, who is suddenly expected to lead the people side of change for a technology initiative in her organization. She relies on experienced project management partners, team leaders, and a change management consultant to assist her in preparing individuals in her workplace for change.

Following each narrative section, there is guidance on why we are taking each step, questions to help you reflect on readiness, and tools you can use in preparing for change. My goal in using this narrative structure is to illustrate the concepts with a real-world scenario, based on the many projects I've been a part of over the years. The narrative will make the information easy to understand and apply in a realistic way. Because in the real world, tools, initiatives and events overlap and happen simultaneously, rather than in a neatly structured sequence. As our lead character discovers, there are many ways to approach change. Focus on preparation and readiness can simplify and accelerate technology adoption. This, in turn, improves our implementations and results in successful change.

Organizational Change Management and the READY-Set-Change Model

Elizabeth slammed her laptop shut and sighed at the stack of papers next to her. "How do they expect me to do this when I'm not even sure about what we're doing!" She scowled at the project plan on top of the mound of papers. Elizabeth was the Human Resources manager of a mid-sized health system undergoing constant change. The IT department seemed to have all the project managers working on a new Electronic Medical Record (EMR) system, so Elizabeth had been assigned the job of overseeing change management for a Document Management Imaging System, a big component of the EMR implementation.

She'd gone to a session on Organizational Change Management at a conference and had told her boss Tom about her interest. Now she was stuck overseeing change management on a project that she didn't know much about.

"That's what I get for sharing my excitement about change management," she laughed at herself. Her talent management and recruiting teams were experienced and didn't need constant supervision, so she didn't have an excuse not to help with the Document Management Imaging System project.

Elizabeth googled "Organizational Change Management" and was immediately sorry. The pages and pages of search results were overwhelming. She found the handout from the presentation she'd attended. It had a big list of deliverables, but she wasn't sure if she needed all of them or even what they were. She'd been thinking about going to training to learn more, but now she didn't have time. This change was happening right away!

Just as she was starting to panic, she got a text from Jake, her best friend and a project manager in IT. "Coffee?" He was one of the project leaders for the Electronic Medical Record project. Jake was working on helping the outpatient clinics prepare for the Electronic Medical Record and he had a dedicated change management consultant on his team.

She texted back, "YES! 3pm?" To herself, she thought, ""Maybe he can help me figure out where to start."

***

"Hey!" Jake called out, "want to run the Harborside half marathon this year?"

Elizabeth rolled her eyes and then felt guilty. She'd been promising to run a race with him for the past four years but hadn't made time to do it. Now he wanted her to run a marathon!

"You know the answer. I haven't even done a 10K, so a marathon is not on the agenda for me," she said.

"It's in five months, so you've got time to prepare. It will be cool," Jake pleaded. "I've already registered for the full marathon, and you only need to get up to half that. We'll train together at lunch or after work. C'mon, no more excuses."

Elizabeth felt a small flicker of interest. It would be good to have a challenge and a distraction from her personal life, and she needed to incorporate more exercise into her increasingly sedentary life.

"I'll think about it," she promised, half-hoping he'd forget. "By the way, do you think your change management consultant can meet with me to talk about my new project? I'm not sure where to begin." Elizabeth filled Jake in on her new assignment.

"I'll make you a deal," he said, "you bring your shoes and workout stuff to run with me tomorrow, and I'll set up a meeting for you and Allie, the consultant."

Elizabeth had to laugh at Jake's persistence. It was almost annoying, but she did need help. "Deal!" she replied.

The following Tuesday, as Elizabeth waited for Allie and Jake, she moved gingerly to the closest chair in the small conference room. She'd been running two or three miles a day with Jake for nearly a week, but she was still sore and stiff most days. Allie and Jake arrived together, neither of them looking like they were in pain. Elizabeth tried not to wince as she moved her chair for them to take their seats.

"Jake tells me you're working on the Document Management Imaging System. It's an important project to get us ready for the EMR. How can I help?"

"Well, I don't know much about leading a change like this, but I've heard that projects fail because teams focus on the technology and forget the people," Elizabeth said.

Allie nodded. "Yes, happens all the time! That's why I changed my focus from Project Management to Change Management. Stakeholders and end users need preparation for change. Without it they're at risk of becoming frustrated, hopeless, or negative."

"I know how that feels," Elizabeth sighed. "When our new Learning Management System was implemented, I got an email

telling me about it the day it went live! I didn't even know the project was underway. I was so frustrated that I started looking for another position. I couldn't believe no one had thought to tell me about such a massive change for my area!" Elizabeth realized she was nearly shouting. *"Sorry, I guess I'm still upset about it,"* she admitted.

"That's understandable. The goal is to make sure people are aware of and ready for the change." Allie continued, *"One of the reasons projects fail is a lack of preparation for those who'll be using and benefiting from the new program. Organizational Change Management simply means helping an organization and its stakeholders move from the current state to a future state, basically from where we are to where we need to be. Organizations that prepare people for change, especially technology change, have a higher rate of success with projects. It sounds simple, but it's not easy,"* Allie warned.

"Just like our marathon!" Jake chimed in.

"Don't remind me," groaned Elizabeth, *"I'm sore and tired, and we've only made it about three miles in training!"*

Allie laughed, *"Jake's right, though. It's like a marathon in the sense that you need time to prepare. You can't decide to make a change one day, implement it the next day, and expect people to be successful using it. We need time to prepare, to build strength and endurance, and to check everyone's progress on how ready they are for the event."*

"Okay, I get it, but where do I start?" Elizabeth asked.

"I'm working on a change management approach and plan for the EMR project. I recommend you use the READY-Set-Change Model. The model is a simple framework and fits technology change. You can think of it as the difference between preparing for a 10K and running a marathon," Allie teased.

"Can we make that the difference between a 5K and a marathon?" Elizabeth asked Jake. "A 5K is a better target for me, and something I can actually accomplish. This marathon is really too much for me since I'm not a runner. I'm a neophyte, and an aching one at that!"

"I get it," Jake sighed. "We can train together, but I'll need a different training plan to prepare for the marathon. You can work on your speed and maybe set your sights on trying a 10K?"

"Whew!" Elizabeth exclaimed. "This meeting has been a relief for me. I can use the READY-Set-Change Model to help prepare people for the new Document Management System. And now I'm only on the hook for a 5K," she looked at Jake and quickly added, "with a stretch goal of a 10K. I made out really well! Now, if I could just stand up without my hamstrings objecting, I'd say this was an excellent meeting!"

Change can be technological, involving a computer system or upgrade; programmatic, such as the introduction of a new health care program; or cultural, like merging two companies or departments into one. The growing recognition that Organizational

Change Management (OCM) is an important and necessary component to successfully implement projects and changes has increased the demand for an organized approach to change.

Using Organizational Change Management helps people adapt to a new way of working or adopt a new system. The change is more successful and less stressful. People return to being productive more quickly than if we don't use a thoughtful approach to change. OCM used to be considered a "nice-to-have" component of a project, but it's become apparent is that change management is a "must-have" to ensure the people side of change is recognized.

After beginning my career in training and development, I pursued a master's degree in communications. I discovered I loved working with leaders on developing their leadership skills, which included crafting messages and stories to engage and enlist others in pursuit of a vision or goal. In working with leaders, I would often facilitate sessions to help redesign processes. I was able to use training and communication skills to help others identify why a process wasn't working. My clients appreciated that I could help redesign the process in question through a collaborative approach.

I hadn't heard the term Organizational Change Management until I was offered a role as a change management lead for a large project. When the team described the role as communications, training and process redesign, I knew I'd found my niche. I began to learn all I could about change management. I attended conferences, trainings, and seminars and voraciously read books by change management leaders like John Kotter and Daryl Conner. I quickly learned that the success of any change is measured through business results and outcomes. A question to ask is "What percentage of the success of this project will be determined by the acceptance and use of the change by the business?"

The goal of OCM is to help stakeholders adopt and use the change to benefit the organization. The benefits of change vary with the project and are usually identified by leadership as the reason to pursue change. Benefits may be described as positive financial outcomes, productivity improvements, integration of multiple systems, or enhanced user experience. This means that if we know what we expect as an outcome and we can help others change the way they do things to meet that outcome, our change is successful.

More than two decades after my first change management role, I still use skills I developed during that project. I've been experimenting, defining, and refining how to provide an understandable and easy-to-follow approach to help people prepare for and adopt change. The results of my desire to make implementations – particularly technology projects – easier and more productive and to get the business back to business is what I've provided here with the READY-Set-Change Model.

OCM Leads to Long-term Success

My first big Organizational Change Management project was a large Enterprise Resource Planning (ERP) project at a Big Ten University. An ERP combines the work that is in separate systems into one system for the entire enterprise. The goal is to integrate information so that it is to manage and understand.

At this university, there were 23 schools and colleges, and each used their own individual databases to conduct business. This meant that every time a faculty or staff member wanted information about someone outside of their school, college, or unit, they had to either make a phone call and ask the other unit for information or, if they were lucky, they could log in to another college's system. For example, the Law School would have to call the College of Engineering to verify a student's information. In this world of separate databases, students and employees had to provide all their personal information to each school or college as well as to departments such as Admissions, Advising, and Financials.

Current State: Separate Databases

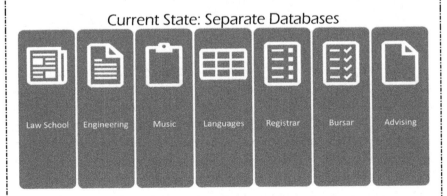

Law School | Engineering | Music | Languages | Registrar | Bursar | Advising

Our charge was to eliminate all these separate databases and to have faculty, staff, and students in one enterprise-wide

system, which would create and maintain one record for each individual. This would allow all of the schools, colleges, and departments to interact with that one record, eliminating duplicate and inaccurate data across the university.

Future State: With ERP

This project included functionality for Financials (student accounts, accounts payable, accounts receivable, procurement, and budgeting), Student Administration (recruiting, admissions, academic advising, scheduling, and grades reports), Human Resources (recruiting, hiring, payroll, time and leave, expenses and retirement information), Research (pre- and post-award grant management), and Space Inventory (management of all campus buildings and locations).

The project's visionary leader could see that this level of change was not going to be easy for the university. To manage this level of change, we needed an OCM methodology, which was led by our implementation partner, Anderson Consulting (now Accenture). My background in communications, training and development, customer experience and process redesign was an excellent match for the skills needed in Organizational Change Management.

Identifying a strategy on how to connect with the stakeholders, including faculty and staff, developing tools to help end users and stakeholders prepare for the change, and crafting tips and techniques to support the end users and stakeholders through the change made our extremely complex project successful. This success extended beyond the system implementation to include process optimization after the initial adoption period.

READY-Set-Change Reflections

1. What types of technology changes have you personally had to adopt in the past?

2. How did you know about this change?

3. Did you fully understand how the change would impact you?

4. Do you feel you were ready for the change? If not, why not?

What Is Readiness?

The next morning, as Elizbeth towel dried her hair, she looked at the clock. "At least five minutes," she thought, as she turned on the blow dryer. Drying her hair was one of her least favorite parts of the day, and she always tried to shortcut the process. But when she didn't spend enough time drying her hair, she found little curls and knots would spring up wherever they chose all over her head. "Seems like what happens when we don't spend enough time helping people get ready for change. We run into knots and tangles everywhere!" The five minutes passed slowly, and her mind wandered to her own experience of getting and being ready.

She didn't like the time it to took prepare for work. Her natural tendency was to jump right into a situation and figure it out as she went along. Knowing that she wasn't particularly good at being ready for things herself, she sure didn't feel ready to lead this initiative and help other people prepare for change. Readiness had eluded Elizabeth in her own life. She would sometimes focus on a goal, such as planting a garden or working out before work, but she often found that she hadn't spent enough time on the preparation phase. She would typically end up frustrated when she couldn't reach her goal. Her garden went untended last summer. The carrots and lettuce disappeared into a field of weeds. Her attempts to get herself in shape by going to the gym before work had failed, due to disorganized mornings that descended into chaos as she herded her kids to school.

Other areas of her life were also in chaos. Elizabeth's husband had asked for a divorce recently and was already seeing someone else. She felt helpless, heartbroken, and worried about their two sons and how they'd adjust. She wasn't ready to tell anyone at work yet.

She thought about her new goal, preparing for the race with Jake. She didn't want to let him down, but worried she was in over her head. She didn't particularly enjoy running. But since she needed both a distraction and some exercise, she grabbed her shorts and shoes on her way out the door.

*****

During their scheduled lunchtime training run, Elizabeth panted while trying to keep pace with Jake, who was increasing his speed. "I mentioned using the READY-Set-Change Model to my boss, Tom," she *reported with labored breaths. "He was really excited and said it was exactly what we need. And Allie sent me an invitation for a Change Management kick-off meeting for your project." Cutting a corner short, Elizabeth asked, "Are you going to that meeting?"*

"Yes, I saw the agenda. Anyone involved in leading change management for a project should attend. I think Allie will be educating the entire group on strategy, recognizing benefits, and tools we'll need to lead change." Jake picked up his speed again, leaving Elizabeth scrambling to catch up.

"I hope she'll help me move quickly. My project is going live soon, and I feel anything but ready!" Elizabeth admitted. She suddenly wondered why she'd bothered with her hair this morning, as she realized she'd be needing another shower.

Let's face it, some people have an easier time than others preparing for and adjusting to change. Everyone goes through changes in life, some larger than others. But the experience of initial resistance, confusion, learning, adapting, and finally adopting a change is relatively universal.

Readiness is the extent to which employees are ready, willing, and able to adopt change and is a key indicator of project success. The READY-Set-Change Model complements traditional Organizational Change Management, with an intense focus on advanced preparation and integrated support to ensure that business objectives are met.

The READY-Set-Change Model focuses on preparation and awareness: how ready, willing and able people are to move through and adopt change. A key feature of the approach is the READY-Set-Change Model which is tactical and practical, to simplify and accelerate the change process as end users and stakeholders move to adoption more quickly.

The READY-Set-Change Model works well with Agile methodology, which many project teams used to plan, execute, and evaluate the outcome of the project through short "sprints," or iterations. At the end of each sprint, the team collaborates with stakeholders to evaluate the outcome or product and to identify adjustments needed in the next sprint. Continuous improvement is the goal of each iteration at every stage. The READY-Set-Change Model is an easy framework for quickly testing and revising information and activities in an ongoing iterative cycle. Technology projects that follow an Agile approach (one of multiple sprints, iteration, feedback, rework, and continued sprints) are perfect candidates for the READY-Set-Change Model.

Enabling the business to use an application or system before it is perfected, while it's still in development, can provide needed exposure to start building knowledge, flexibility, and muscle memory. This improves the implementation's success. Of course, allowing users to participate in agile iterations also depends on the users' understanding of the process. Otherwise, they may become frustrated with constantly changing interfaces and functionality. Involving the technical team with the business as they work through scenarios adds information and understanding for both groups.

In technology projects, there is a defined future state. Those who will be using the technology can see what it will look like after implementation. In an organizational change such as a merger or reorganization, planned job changes or reassignments may not be visible to those impacted.

Preparing people for change with the READY-Set-Change Model mitigates the risk of negativity and lost productivity in the transition from current to future state.

What is Readiness?

While it may seem as though "prepared" and "ready" are synonymous, I believe there is a subtle distinction between the terms. Being "prepared" refers to having done work in advance so that when an event occurs there is a plan in place to ensure things run smoothly. Being "ready," however, seems to have an emotional component. For example, consider a medical procedure such as a surgery. The medical team is *prepared* for the surgery. They have studied the techniques and have all the necessary tools and specialists on hand. The medical team may still be nervous and unsure about whether the surgery will go well. They may feel they're not *ready*, even though they are prepared. As a patient, I want to make sure my medical team is both prepared and ready!

Developing a READY mindset is an important tool in a work environment that is **V**olatile, **U**ncertain, **C**omplex, and **A**mbiguous (VUCA). Change is constant, and most people are dealing with multiple changes at one time. A READY mindset is agile and flexible, with an understanding that what is one way today, may quickly change. A READY mindset recognizes that our job is to be ready to flex our skills, patience, and ability to quickly respond to a shifting landscape.

The Power of Muscle Memory

An example of the demands of change was evident when I worked on an enterprise-wide system change for a government agency. The end users had been using an old "green-screen" or DOS system for nearly 20 years. In that system, users navigated with function keys, such as F3 or F9, to get to the appropriate screen to enter data or find information.

The new enterprise system had a menu-based user interface (as almost all 21st century systems have), meaning it was more like Salesforce, Amazon, and other menu driven applications. The users would navigate with a mouse and menus rather than entering F-key commands on the keyboard. This was a massive change for the users of the system, both mentally and physically. They were used to a physical rhythm using the function and tab keys to move through the fields. The rhythm of F keys and Tabs was how users quickly managed information. The new system, mouse- and menu-driven, meant users had to look at the screen and navigate to the correct field visually rather than use a familiar sequence of keystrokes.

The training provided by the technology vendor was insufficient. It focused on the type of information that could be entered in each field, rather than how people would do their jobs using the new system. The productivity loss, frustration, and lack of interest in using the system could have been easily prevented. Instead, the project team could have observed end users who were entering invoices or purchase order information. They could have then sped up the learning process by creating specific keyboard shortcuts, job aids, and tips-based training. They could also have accelerated adoption by creating a data entry user group throughout the organization.

> *Changing the physical interaction with a system takes time. Developing a plan to harness the power of muscle memory really helps people move more quickly to a new process.*

Athletes, actors, musicians, and others who perform must practice daily to keep their muscle memory tightly tuned. It's the only way to stay conditioned and ready.

Tennis champion Billie Jean King maintained a relentless focus on a READY mindset. In 1973, she was given an opportunity to change the perception of women in sports when she received an invitation to play a match against male tennis champion Bobby Riggs. Bobby was twice her age, but a formidable opponent. Billie Jean carefully considered the offer and weighed several options for response. She recognized that even though she was in peak physical condition, she needed to spend time to become truly ready for the match. She agreed to play Bobby Riggs and began to prepare for this challenge.

In the weeks leading up to the match, which was now being billed as the "Battle of the Sexes," Riggs courted the media, providing interview after interview to anyone who asked. This left him with little time to practice and prepare. King, on the other hand, spent that time studying videos of Bobby's matches and developing her strategy. Most importantly, she decided that she would adjust in any way necessary to be ready to win. On October 20, 1973, Billie Jean King prevailed in the winner-take-all match, earning $100,000. What's more, she commanded new respect for women by beating him in three straight sets, a 6-4, 6-3, 6-3 victory. How did she manage such an upset? She was *ready.*

Preparation is the first step of readiness. Most workplaces require annual drills for fires, tornados, or even earthquakes. The reason for these drills is to prepare and be ready when an event occurs. Practicing how to vacate a building or take cover prepares us to respond if there's an emergency. The emotional acceptance that an emergency will occur helps to be truly ready.

Readiness is essential to adapting quickly. Workplace change, such as a team member moving to another position or leaving, can wreak havoc on our work. Reassignment, added responsibility, and matrixed roles also change our work and may even lead to opportunity. If you're ready to step into more responsibility and have been practicing readiness, you'll be comfortable moving into a more visible or higher position. But if you haven't prepared, your lack of readiness might impede your ability to be successful in a larger role.

Readiness as a practice is a continuous evaluation of where you are currently, an evolution of where you'd like to go, and the preparation to get there. Top athletes spend most of their lives pursuing readiness. They practice, receive coaching, and play scrimmage games for additional preparation. Athletes don't just practice their sport, they workout to improve muscle strength and agility. Change readiness requires consistency, which requires discipline.

READY-Set-Change Reflections

1. Do you have a personal or professional challenge that you want to conquer?

2. How are you becoming ready to meet this challenge?

3. Have you visualized what you will do and how you will do it?

4. Do you feel you are ready to take on this challenge? If not, why not?

The READY-Set-Change Model

When Elizabeth arrived at the coffee shop, she saw Allie and Jake were waiting for her. Getting out of the office was always a treat for Elizabeth. Today's visit was even better, because Elizabeth was looking forward to understanding the READY-Set-Change Model. She was excited to begin drafting her plan for the project.

"Okay," Allie started, "I've discovered through trial and error as well as research that successful adoption of change requires a five-step process. I use the word READY to remind myself of the five steps for successful implementation."

Elizabeth shot a glance at Jake, expecting him to roll his eyes. She was surprised to find him straight-faced and taking notes.

"Go for it!" he said.

....

In my experience with change projects, I've observed firsthand the focus and teamwork it takes to design, develop, test, and implement systems and programs. On technology implementations, the technical and project management teams are usually in sync and have frequent communication with each other about deliverables and progress. But unless there is a dedicated change management resource on the project team, stakeholders who are impacted by the technology change are often an afterthought.

Time and time again, I've needed a fast and simple way to help prepare stakeholders and end users for change That's why I developed the READY-Set-Change Model.

The advantage of the READY-Set-Change Model is that it can be deployed at any point in a project. You won't be surprised to hear, though, that the earlier you use the READY-Set-Change Model in your project, the greater the likelihood of successful adoption. People need to see and hear a message at least nine to sixteen times before they fully understand and recognize the impact it will have on them.[5] So, the greater the lead time on messaging the better! Engaging the

---

[5] Gallup, Inc, Gallup. "State of the American Workplace." Gallup.com, Gallup, 12 Dec. 2019, www.gallup.com/workplace/238085/state-american-workplace-report-2017.aspx

organization's leaders also takes time and is critically important in driving change and successful adoption. So even though the model can be used at any point, I'm not recommending that you wait. Rather, I recognize that our readiness and change efforts are often started much later than optimal. Yet we still must do all we can to help stakeholders and end users prepare for, adopt, and sustain the behavioral changes necessary for successful adoption.

To use the READY-Set-Change Model, you must have a deep understanding of why the change is happening. You'll use this understanding to develop the rest of the tools for implementation:

R   **Relevant and relatable** messaging about the change

E   **Engage leaders** as sponsors and actively promote the change

A   **Advance** communication to ensure messaging is received, and **Advocating** for stakeholders

D   **Develop support** for and training on process and technology

Y   Reinforce **WHY** and reduce resistance to adoption

In the years I've been deploying this model, the flexibility of it has been an advantage. Many of the activities can be performed simultaneously, meaning there is no need to wait for the relevant and relatable messaging to be complete before engaging leaders and sponsors. Developing the support plan and training can happen at the same time as advance communication is occurring.

Using the READY-Set-Change Model allows you to promote, prepare, and move people to readiness in a simple manner and at an accelerated pace. Together, these factors greatly enhance project success.

Elizabeth resisted the urge to quip, "I'm ready!" and instead opened a new file on her laptop.

Allie continued, "These steps work especially well with technology change, and I'll explain why as we work through each one."

*"**R** is for **Relevant and Relatable**, meaning that to help people get ready for change, we need to make sure they understand what is changing and why. We usually talk about software or system changes in technical terms. In fact, many technology projects are named for the software they're using, such as SAP or Workday or some acronym," Allie sighed.*

"Like DMIS," Jake smirked.

"Yes," said Allie, "we should be talking about the benefit or purpose of a project in a way that humans can understand! Sorry, this is my BPP, biggest pet peeve!" Allie grinned.

Every project or initiative needs a name that's easy to understand and that describes the purpose or goal in a clear and accessible way. Go further by creating relevant examples to describe how things will change. Using metaphor, analogy and story to connect to specific audiences is essential to ensure those who will be impacted by the change truly understand it. If creative communication is not your strength, enlist the help of creative types, such as your organization's Communications or Marketing team.

*"**E** is to **Engage Leaders**," continued Allie. "Leadership engagement is critical to success, and we have different types of leaders. We have sponsors who are responsible and accountable for the change, plus our CEO and front-line leaders. This must be a true partnership. Elizabeth, when you've figured out the relevant and relatable messaging, you should bring your sponsor, Darren, up to speed, so he can reinforce the messaging. Discussing with the team will help engage him and make meeting with him as a partner easier."*

"I'm nervous about keeping him involved. He gets busy and tends to lose focus because he has so much on his plate," Elizabeth frowned.

"It's good you're aware of his tendency to lose focus. We'll help you plan how to keep him informed," Allie reassured her.

Many sponsors find it hard to stay focused on promoting change due to the amount of information and the number of changes they find themselves involved in. It's often necessary to remind sponsors of their role and of the importance of promoting the change with their teams. This may involve giving them ready-to-send messages or instructions for specific activities. When sponsors know what is expected and needed from them, it's easier for them to stay visible and active in promoting the change.

*Allie continued her lesson by saying, "**A** is for **Advance and Advocate**.".*

Jake stopped writing and looked up. "That sounds weird. What's that mean exactly?" he asked.

"Advance refers to advance communication. It's simply a way of saying that we need to get communication out to our stakeholders and end users in advance. We don't wait until a week before we go live to let people know about a change. And we don't just send an email and consider communication done.

"A lot of projects fail because of little and late communication, which can happen for several reasons. Sometimes the team is trying to get all the communication perfect before they let anyone know about the change. Other times they need approval and can't get it before sending out. When we hesitate, it's too late. We doom ourselves without advance communication," Allie advised.

"Remember the new timekeeping system last year?" Jake asked Elizabeth. Elizabeth's face grew hot as she suddenly realized she'd been the one who'd held up advance communication. It was the biggest complaint they'd heard: no advance warning that something as significant as timekeeping was changing. Elizabeth nodded her head, hoping he wouldn't notice her embarrassment. She changed the subject by asking Allie, "And what do you mean by 'advocate'?"

"Well," said Allie, "we must advocate for the change throughout the organization. If we hear misinformation or negativity about the change, it's important to address it, and then promote and advocate for the change. I like to provide communication tools such as a webpage and 'Frequently Asked Questions.' These help leaders support and advocate for the change."

"Got it," said Jake.

"There's a second role in advocacy though," continued Allie. "Effective advocates stay connected to the technical and project teams to make sure decisions are made with the end users and stakeholders in mind.

"If there's an issue that's expensive to fix or needs more time and money than is available, the project or technical team might add a manual step, such as expecting users to log in to another system to find information. They may not realize the difficulty that extra step creates for end users or stakeholders.

"As change practitioners, it's our responsibility to advocate for the stakeholder and end user. We have to explain how logging out to perform a task in another system, and then logging back in to complete their work, will frustrate and aggravate users." Allie paused to give Jake and Elizabeth time to process what they'd heard.

"Is this like when you have to go out of our expense submittal process and scan receipts into a different system, save it as a PDF, and then upload the PDF to the new expense system?" Jake asked.

"Exactly!" Allie nodded.

"Well, it was supposed to be all in one system," Elizabeth pointed out, "but there was a problem with integrating the scanning with the expenses. I know they want to fix it someday..." She trailed off.

"Yes! This is exactly what we're talking about. No one wants these issues, but sometimes people are more flexible than technology.

Technical issues are sometimes renamed 'training issues' and expected to be solved by people. That's why advocating for those in the business is an important part of this work," Allie said.

"I'm sorry, but I've got to get across town for a meeting. Can we resume this conversation tomorrow at 7:30?" asked Jake.

"Same here," said Elizabeth.

"Of course," Allie replied. "Between now and then, look for examples of people filling the gap for technology. Once you start looking, you'll see these examples everywhere."

Advocacy is defined as the act of supporting a cause or proposal. In the READY-Set-Change Model, advocacy is two-sided. On one side, advocacy is for the change itself. The flip side is advocating for the stakeholders and users.

By putting a focus on advocacy for the change, we recognize that it would be impossible for every person to be engaged, enthused, or happy about every change project. Sometimes the project is disruptive to another area in the organization. Yet, supporting the direction of the organization is an important responsibility of leaders and sponsors.

Stakeholders are everyone impacted by the change, including those who never touch or see the system. Users are those who will be interacting with the system, which means they are stakeholders, but with direct access and different needs.

Support for the stakeholders is necessary for successful change. Using the READY-Set-Change Model requires change practitioners to express concern, propose alternatives, and support adjustments to make sure users and stakeholders are not forgotten.

··

The next morning, Jake was unloading a box of donut holes and distributing coffee. "Sorry I'm late, but it's your fault, Allie. I went to get donuts and saw an example of the gap we talked about yesterday."

"Really? What happened?" asked Elizabeth.

"Well, I thought it'd be faster to go into the donut shop than wait in the drive-thru. I gave the guy at the counter my order and he printed out the order on two small slips of paper. He stuck one slip on the donut case, and then put the other slip of paper on the coffee counter, next to the drive-thru window. The drive-thru orders were showing up on a screen as they're entered by the drive-thru team. I asked my guy why the inside orders were printed on paper and the drive thru-orders were on the screen. He shrugged and said they didn't know how to get all the orders from the counter and drive-thru on the screen together, so they had to use paper.

"My donut order was filled quickly. But I could see that my coffee order slip was sitting on the counter, being ignored by the busy drive-thru team. Finally, after five minutes, my patience ran out. I kind of demanded the coffee, which led to an emergency with everyone getting mad at each other for not remembering to fill the paper order for coffee. Is that what you're talking about? They needed someone to advocate for them?" Jake looked like he was expecting a pat on the head.

"Exactly," said Allie. "Because a technical solution couldn't be managed, people are trying to make up the difference. The situation you ran into probably happens many times each day, with the crew getting more and more frustrated each time it happens. That's why mismanaged change often creates a negative workplace." Then, remembering Jake's opening remark, she added, "But why is this my fault?"

"Before, I'd have just figured the entire staff was incompetent. But now I see the challenges of an automated and manual system are what's creating the problem. And it's your fault that I know that!" Jake teased.

Allie rolled her eyes at Elizabeth, who was getting impatient.

"What does the D stand for?" Elizabeth asked.

"Donuts," answered Jake, to more eyerolls from his colleagues.

Allie took a sip of her coffee. "D is **Develop support** and ensure readiness with training."

"Do you mean training and development?" Elizabeth asked. "In our HR department, the training and development area is one of our Centers of Excellence But they usually work on leadership and supervisory skills training. Is that what you are talking about? Training people on new skills and developing their capabilities?"

"Sort of," replied Allie. "Developing support and ensuring readiness are crucial to assisting people as they adjust to and adopt new technology and processes. Training focuses on developing capability in the individual, on how to do their jobs with the new system and new processes. Developing support means creating capacity within the organization itself."

"Like what?" asked Jake.

"Providing access to real help and ongoing training on specific tasks after go-live is a great way to support users with the change." Allie continued, "Development to sustain change includes creating superuser groups, reviewing and updating training materials, supporting a robust help desk, and developing job aids. All these ideas and more can improve the adoption of change."

"That seems like a lot of effort," Jake said. "Can't we just show people how the system works, and let them figure out the rest?"

"Hmmm," said Elizabeth, "are you saying I don't need to train for our race? Should I just show up and see what happens?"

"Okay, I get it," Jake laughed.

"Working with stakeholders and users on tools they need, is one way to provide support for people on how to do their jobs in the new world," Allie advised.

"Hey," said Elizabeth, "what about the HR changes that might happen? You know when we change someone's job significantly, we've got to reclassify them with a title or grade change. We need to get HR involved!"

"Consider yourself involved," Jake said as he stood up and headed out.

"Oh, wow! I'm not sure we're ready for readiness," Elizabeth murmured, making a note to meet with her HR Team.

The first few weeks after a change can be difficult for users and other stakeholders. Development of a go-live and ongoing support plan to help them goes a long way toward successfully sustaining change. Without an ongoing support plan, users often feel abandoned and may not be sure where to turn for help. Developing a superuser community can begin during the User Acceptance Testing phase of a project. This helps ensure the superusers are identified, prepared, and ready to assist those who need help and ongoing support.

"Ok, why do we need Y?" Jake asked.

"**Y** is **Why,**" Allie explained. Seeing Jake's confusion, she added, "as in the word, W-H-Y. When we use the READY-Set-Change Model, we know we need to keep sharing the 'why' of the change. 'Why' is our purpose, and sharing it reduces resistance."

"Why resistance?" Jake winked at Elizabeth, who was getting annoyed with him.

"Isn't resistance to change natural? I think there are good reasons to resist change sometimes," argued Elizabeth, thinking about her personal situation.

"I agree," said Allie, "and yet resistance must be addressed to help adopt change, especially change we can't control."

Understanding the "WHY" is an essential foundation for organizations. Author Simon Sinek defines our WHY as "Why we do, not what we do."[6] It drives behavior. When developing your relevant and relatable messaging, incorporate the WHY. While you're working on the advance communication, incorporate your WHY. And, as you develop a support plan, keep the WHY in mind. Reinforcing the WHY for your users and stakeholders reminds them of their purpose. When we're facing resistance, we must bring people back to the WHY of the organization and of the change. This will help them move through the discomfort and frustration of change.

"Please tell me you can help me use the READY-Set-Change Model," Elizabeth groaned. *"I'm not sure where to begin."*

"No problem," assured Allie. "We'll begin with the kickoff meeting. Keep your eyes and ears open for Relevant and Relatable examples and stories we can use to describe the change."

---

[6] Sinek, S. (2009). Start with why: How great leaders get everyone on the same page. New York: Portfolio.

Relevant and Relatable

Allie began the Change Management Kick-off meeting by saying, "Essentially, the goal of Organizational Change Management is to ensure that stakeholder adoption and utilization are successful in order to reap the benefits of the change." Elizabeth noticed several team members pulled out their phones to check email.

"Now, before you all stop listening to me, let me give you a 'jargon-free' version of that statement," Allie continued. "All change must have some sort of benefit, or we wouldn't be doing it. For example, I'm moving to a new house in three weeks. It's a really big change for my family, but there are clear benefits to moving, even though it's difficult to pack and get ready. Some of the benefits are a great school for my daughter, and three bedrooms, so my son and daughter won't have to share anymore. It's close enough to work for my husband to ride his bike and save on gas and parking fees. My favorite part, though, is the big backyard with space for a garden. I've been wanting a garden longer than I can remember. So, I've clearly identified the benefits of this change."

"Yeah, and it's something you've chosen," John said. John was the PMO manager and had told Elizabeth on several occasions that people should just do their jobs and stop being frustrated by what they couldn't control. He added, "When we've got change at work, we don't get to choose."

Allie seemed surprised to hear John pointing out this lack of choice. "You're right," she agreed. "Lack of choice or not having control does frustrate us. That's why it's our job as change leaders to clearly communicate the benefits in a way people can understand." She continued, "I think it's also important to identify what people will lose with change. Even when you know the benefits, and even if you have a choice, there are losses.

"In my case," Allie admitted, "when we leave our current house, we'll miss our fantastic neighbors who are more like family than friends. And the neighborhood park with playground equipment. I'll even miss the reading nook upstairs, though I don't find time to use it." Allie shrugged, and it was obvious the nostalgia was getting the best of her.

"Acknowledging loss is hard for us. But when we're helping people accept change, it's important to acknowledge all aspects of change. We can't just pretend that there aren't any losses."

Elizabeth noticed that all phones had been put aside, and the entire group was listening intently to Allie.

Allie continued, "Our goal is to have our stakeholders, which include end users, choose and use the change. When they do, the benefit we are hoping for from the change happens. For example, if my change is successful, my daughter will like having her own room, enjoy school, and make new friends. We'll see the benefits of the move. If, on the other hand, she wants to room with her brother, and misses her old friends so much that she begs to go back and play with them or doesn't make new friends, we'll have a lack of adoption. We won't get the benefits of the change."

"She'll get over it," said John. "Just don't drive her to see the old friends." John chuckled at his own comment.

"But," Elizabeth was surprised to find herself speaking up, "this happens all the time when we make changes at work. Someone turns off the old system or tells us our spreadsheet is gone! It happens really quickly with technology change, and we barely have any notice!" Elizabeth looked down at her notepad, embarrassed by her outburst.

Allie nodded her head in agreement. "The goal is to identify the benefits and share them in a relevant and relatable way to anyone who will be impacted. Knowing why, when, and what we'll get from changing is important.

"As we build out our change management plan for the EMR, I'll share the progress Elizabeth makes with the READY-Set-Change Model.

Let's begin to identify benefits of the EMR. Elizabeth, feel free to join in and share your DMIS ideas."

Elizabeth was hopeful when the meeting adjourned an hour later. She had started to figure out relevant and relatable ideas about her project.

A relevant and relatable message highlights the benefit of the change for those who are impacted, such as employees, stakeholders, and leaders. This messaging is critical to the success of any change initiative. With technology change, it's even more important, because the technical team and project teams are used to using technology jargon as a part of their language. To everyone else affected by the change, these acronyms and technical terms are meaningless, or even intimidating.

The goal of relevant and relatable messaging is to help each individual believe the change is worth the trade of time and comfort. Even when there's no choice about moving to a new technology, most of us still make this trade in our minds. Will the discomfort of the new be offset by the benefit I receive? Sometimes it is a clear yes!

On a recent project an entire organization had to upgrade their operating system to a newer version. The version they were using was no longer supported and the new operating system would provide features they didn't currently have. People were not very interested in taking the time to train on the new operating system though. But, when they learned the new operating system would increase the speed of processing and the new features would eliminate some manual workarounds, most people recognized the benefits of the change were worth the time it would take to learn and adopt the new system.

In cases where the gain or benefit is longer term and not immediately apparent, it's helpful to figure out how to give some immediate reward to keep momentum going.

Recognizing and developing a description of the benefits of change helps people get ready. Translate the benefits and the technology change to "kitchen-English," acronym-free, clear language you'd use to talk with someone in your kitchen. No jargon or labels, just common terms and examples.

An example of the importance of a relevant and relatable name and elimination of jargon was evident on a project called MICAM. The old Single Sign-On system was being replaced with an advanced technology that would allow access to all systems and applications for both government employees and the general public. The working name being used by the technical teams was MICAM, Michigan Credentialing and Access Management.

This was for the state of Michigan, and because the abbreviation for Michigan is MI (pronounced MY) it seemed that all systems were called MI something. MICAM for Michigan Credentialing and Access Management didn't explain what the project would accomplish, and it didn't really roll off the tongue.

The purpose of the system was to help people log in to all of their systems at once. So we changed the name to MILogin. MI for the State of Michigan, and Login, referring to the goal of logging in to all applicable systems.

I love our technical teams and respect all they do, but they shouldn't have the last word about what to call systems or projects. The end users who will use the system and the stakeholders who are impacted don't care that credentialing and access management is different from logging in. "MILogin" clearly describes the *purpose* of the system from the users' perspective, not the *function* of the system from a technical standpoint.

Changing the name from MICAM to MILogin made a big difference to the users and didn't hurt the technical team or the project in any way. In fact, it made the project more visible and understandable to everyone who used MILogin. Descriptive naming can help people understand why change is necessary.

If a name can't be changed, a slogan or tagline might work well for description. Collaborate with the marketing team to name high-visibility systems or high-profile projects. They usually are aware of other projects and can help you find a unique "brand" for your initiative.

Develop examples, stories, and analogies to use with stakeholders and user groups. This makes the change easy to understand. What makes something relevant and relatable to one person or team, will not necessarily work for another. Look for universal themes and common experiences, such as childhood, being a student, pets, parenting. Or consider personal milestones, such as learning to drive or moving to a new home, to create connection. The bigger the organization, the more important it is to create relevant and relatable connections, which lead to understanding.

How One-Stop Shopping Saved the Day!

Relevant, relatable stories and messaging have the power to drive a change forward or leave it shrouded in jargon and double-speak. As a change management lead at a Big Ten University, I helped implement an Enterprise Resource Planning (ERP) system at a time when this was a brand-new concept. This system tracked all financial transactions, including accounting, procurement, budgeting, student registration, academic advising, grading, and graduation, as well as all HR tasks, such as hiring, payroll, benefits, retirement, and leave. The 23 schools, colleges, and units at the University all had separate databases, which required different logins and passwords. Getting information from one point to another required logging in and out of different systems.

My boss was a brilliant technical leader, and one who didn't always understand why others didn't think the way she did. Our first big task was to build a change liaison group to implement the project. We needed department and unit leaders who were high enough in the organization to make decisions, yet still close enough to the day-to-day work to know how things were done. At our first meeting to enlist these change liaisons, my boss drew this image on the whiteboard:

The image, which looked like a barrel or a can of soup, represented a relational database, which was the technical structure of the system. Our change liaisons weren't sure how this relational database related to them. They thought this was a waste of time and left without commitment. We set up a meeting for the following month to try again.

While thinking about how we could explain our new system in a relevant and relatable way, I experienced the frustration of my weekly shopping trip. At the time I had two small daughters, Violet May, age 4, and Emma Rose, age 2. On Saturday mornings we'd run around town to complete our weekly errands. We lived in a small town and had to make many stops. We'd go to the grocery store, the hardware store, the pharmacy, and the bank. At each stop, I had to get the girls out of and then back into their car seats. It was exhausting and aggravating.

I'd heard there was a new Meijer Thrifty Acres store (similar to a Wal-Mart) with "one-stop shopping" about fifteen miles away. Tired of the car seat wrangling, I drove to Meijer the next weekend, and unbuckled and unsnapped the girls. We went in and I was amazed! Meijer had everything we needed under one roof! We could do our grocery shopping, buy lightbulbs, pick up prescriptions, drop off dry cleaning, and go to the bank. Competing our errands all in one place made my life so much easier and cut down on the car seat struggle.

This experience made me think about the struggles our users had, logging in and out of many separate systems, each with a different password, just to get their work completed each day.

I suggested to my boss that we share my experience at Meijer to give an analogy to describe how this system would make the change liaisons' and their teams' lives easier. My boss chuckled at the thought and said, "That's cute, but I'm not comparing our multi-million-dollar system to Meijer." I could see her point.

The following week, when we met with our change liaisons and again drew the database on the board. My boss started to explain to the liaisons how the information from these databases could be accessed, and the liaisons began to gather their things to leave.

"Wait!" she said. "How many of you shop at Meijer?" The liaisons paused, "This new system is like Meijer, and April will tell you why." Now we had their attention!

I explained the hassle of the car seats and how shopping at Meijer had eliminated the car seat struggle. Then related that our new system would be "like Meijer" in the sense that they could go to one place for everything they needed, rather than having to go in and out of multiple systems to complete their work. This analogy made sense to them. The liaisons understood the value of the new system, and the change liaison program was formed. As we moved from design into development, I would often hear our liaisons and stakeholders explaining to each other that decisions they made would either keep our system "like Meijer" or return it to multiple stops to complete a task. Relevant and relatable analogies and stories are keys to helping stakeholders and users understand the vision and purpose of the change.

Stories don't have to be big, important, or particularly dramatic. They simply require an identified problem, attempts to the solve the problem, a hero to help solve the problem, and a lesson. This is an easy-to-use formula, and people listen when you tell them you are going to share a story. They set aside their resistant thinking. This allows them to listen and hopefully glean insights into events that are unfolding.

Identifying Stakeholders and Assessing Their Needs

Identifying the benefit of the change for stakeholders is important. So is recognizing that there are losses associated with the change. Remember, a stakeholder is anyone who has a stake in the change, such as a user of the system or as a partner who will use the outcome in some way.

To deeply understand stakeholders and to make sure your messaging is both relevant and relatable, spend time on stakeholder identification and assessment. As a change professional, I've completed stakeholder assessments for many years. However, my goal to develop a deeper understanding of what drives stakeholder behavior led to the development of the READY-Set-Change Stakeholder Assessment. This tool has sparked deep conversations between the project team, business experts and stakeholders around their experience and expectations. The READY-Set-Change Stakeholder Assessment facilitates discussion with representatives from the business, end users, stakeholders, subject matter experts, project team, and leadership to truly understand what is needed to prepare for change.

Guide the discussion with questions to identify groups of people who will be affected by change and leads discussion to determine the following:

◊ What will this stakeholder group gain from this change?
◊ What will this stakeholder group lose with this change?
◊ What are these stakeholders afraid of as a result of this change?

Discussion develops empathy and understanding of stakeholders. Every change has something to be gained, and some loss, and may create fear for those impacted. The Stakeholder Assessment guides decisions about messaging, outreach, training approach, and ways to sustain change. True adoption of change requires the loss to be identified, and the gain or benefit to be great enough to help stay the course.

Additional questions to develop a deeper and empathic understanding of the needs of stakeholders include:

◇ What is changing in the way they do their job?
◇ Will they use a new system in some way?
◇ Will this initiative change their business process?
◇ Will they need training to do their job differently because of the change?
◇ Do stakeholders and users understand the 'Why' of the change?

To leverage to work involved in identifying the stakeholder groups, such as internal (employees, contractors) and external groups (customers, constituents, partners), and their needs, create a visual stakeholder display to share with the project team and technical team. It can be online or physical, on a white board or a wall. Use stock photos to make a collage of images that represent your stakeholders, their gains, losses, and fears. Naming stakeholder groups, using avatars or personas, is an excellent way to keep the stakeholder assessment results visible and top of mind for the team.

The stakeholder list will continue to evolve. People who were overlooked will emerge. New groups will be identified. Add new stakeholders, plan for them, and keep the project and technical teams updated about new stakeholders.

READY-Set-Change Reflections

1. How have you seen story used in the past to help explain an idea?

2. What resources can you leverage to start stakeholder identification?

3. Can you practice facilitating the stakeholder assessment with the project team? Do they have insights and ideas to add?

4. How will you visually represent your stakeholders to keep them and their concerns in front of the project and technical teams?

READY, Set, Change!

005

Engaging Leaders

"Allie, I'm having a hard time getting my sponsor, Darren, to think about this Document Management Imaging System. It's a really big change for the physicians and their staff, and it may impact patients. Darren is the Chief Operating Officer. He seems to worry about the technology and whether the technology will work. I don't know how to focus his attention on the people and process changes, which are also risk factors." Elizabeth was frustrated, and not sure what to do about her leader's lack of engagement in the project.

"How often do you meet with him?" asked Jake, joining the call.

"Well, I don't have specific meetings to discuss the change aspects of the project. I only see him at team meetings, ut I do talk to him at those. Shouldn't that be enough?" Elizabeth asked.

Allie spoke up , "If you're having trouble engaging the sponsor, in this case Darren, it doesn't sound as if you're meeting with him enough. He may not have a clear understanding of his role. Have you documented sponsor expectations and shared them with Darren? Have you given Darren anything to help clarify sponsor or leader expectations?"

"No. I feel a bit intimidated. He's busy, and I don't want to waste his time. I'm sure he doesn't want me to tell him how to do his job." Elizabeth trailed off.

"I get it," said Allie. "He didn't become a leader without having some experience in promoting change. But imagine if you weren't quite sure what to do to help get everyone ready for a change. Would you appreciate help and ideas on what would be effective?"

"That's why we are on this call," Jake reminded them both.

"Okay, let's think through the different elements of your readiness plan to determine what to share with Darren," Allie continued. "Then we can create a document or checklist of what you'd like him to do to support this change. Of course, you'll adjust as you move along. But having a place to start will help Darren and the entire team prepare."

"That sounds great!" Elizabeth admitted. "Can you help me create this so I can make sure Darren's onboard?"

"Of course," said Allie, "We can work through it together."

"Don't forget about sharing with the EMR team as well," Jake added. "I've got least a half a dozen 'Darrens' to bring up to speed for the EMR project, and I need to engage them to engage everyone else!"

"Will do," said Allie.

"Hanging up now," said Elizabeth. "I need to lead my leader, which means I have a lot to do!"

....

Leaders are responsible for setting direction about priorities and guiding their teams through change. Strong support from at least one executive-level sponsor has a significant impact on project success. Engaging sponsors to communicate the importance of the change increases their effectiveness as leaders.

Sponsors are the leaders who are accountable and responsible for implementing a change. Yet every leader has a responsibility to their teams to keep them informed and aware. Even though essentially all leaders are sponsors of change, all leaders are not necessarily held to the same level of accountability as sponsors.

Sponsors sometimes have difficulty fulfilling their roles due to demands on their time and attention. They are sometimes overstretched in their capacity to lead change. Create an engagement plan, or brief, which identifies activities, messaging, timelines, and ways to engage and show support for the change. Knowing what they can say and do to show their support makes it easy for sponsors. They're happy to have guidance about when to communicate information to end users, encouragement to team members, and updates to the stakeholders.

Engage your sponsor early by giving them a role in the project kickoff. If the sponsor has a well-known interest, it might be possible to tie in a theme for the kickoff for greater engagement. With high-level sponsors, it helps to think of them as big-name actors with a cameo appearance in a TV show or movie. They have an important part to play, but then you want to move back to the action. This keeps the energy high and keeps the program moving. Get creative! Use your sponsors to do video vignettes or other interactive activities, such as a trivia game, rather than to read a PowerPoint presentation.

Be clear and concise with an engagement plan. Rather than asking sponsors and leaders to "message their managers and downline," suggest "Review and personalize email A and send it to your managers on June 1" or "Invite team members to meeting B and add it to their calendars." The change team creates the email or flyer to make it easy for the sponsor to be involved. The more specific and descriptive the task for the sponsor, the more involved they'll become. This ultimately creates readiness for individuals and the organization.

Sponsors must:

◇ Explain why this change is needed and why now
◇ Reassure stakeholders that this is the right direction for the organization
◇ Be positive about the change
◇ Ensure they are visible with frequent communication
◇ Encourage the team, and provide understanding and kudos when the going gets tough
◇ Tell the end users that they are in good hands, and thank them for their patience

By steadily promoting the change and telling it like it is, sponsors and leaders have tremendous impact. Prepare sponsors with messages like, "This may be hard, but we will persevere," or even to change direction quickly if needed.

To build a successful and engaging sponsor relationship:

1. Make sure you meet early and often with the sponsor, don't replace meetings with email
2. Clearly explain your vision for their role and the importance of visibility and support
3. Ask what type of previous experience they've had with sponsoring change
4. Ask about their interests, which can help you develop a relevant and relatable story
5. Clarify how you can help them as a sponsor of change
   ◊ Ask if they'd like you to prepare a Frequently Asked Questions document or if they'd like to collaborate on it
   ◊ Offer to help prepare them for questions and coach them on their responses
6. Provide an example of an engagement plan to determine if there is additional information they'd like to have included or if they prefer a different tool
7. Establish a meeting schedule
   ◊ Schedule a regular cadence of weekly or bi-weekly meetings to keep them current and active
   ◊ Always provide an agenda and action items for sponsors. Think of the action items as the "easy button" for them to be active and visible

8. Create a reporting tool, such as a dashboard, with updated information each month. This report may include:

◇ Sending an awareness survey once a month to measure awareness of the change. For example, you might ask, "Do you know the project will change how you work?"

◇ A quarterly view of technical milestones, with pilot programs and training dates

◇ Updates on other projects or initiatives which might impact people or the change initiative

◇ An update on any new stakeholder groups identified or issues stakeholders may be experiencing

Common Obstacles to Engaging Sponsors

Sometimes it might feel as though you're hitting a brick wall when it comes to engaging and building a relationship with the sponsor. There are any number of roadblocks or obstacles which can get in the way of sponsor engagement.

Not on Board with the Change

Sometimes sponsors know they should be championing a change, but they have their own reservations about this change. They may not have expressed these reservations, but you can see by their lack of engagement that they are not invested or aligned. If you suspect this is the case, ask clarifying questions and see if you can find an area the sponsor is hopeful about. Focus on promoting that aspect of the change.

Distracted by Too Many Projects

When a sponsor doesn't spend as much time as you had planned speaking or engaging with others about change, this can derail the communication and other readiness efforts of the team. This was a frequent issue in a large government agency where we had multiple "top priority" projects. The amount of change was staggering. The sponsor had great intentions, but not great flexibly over schedules, which were often interrupted with legitimate crises. Counterbalance the disrupted focus with a strong yet simple engagement plan. Include a request for a proxy to deliver messages for the sponsor. This allows the change leader to use the sponsor's name in communication. The sponsor can look and feel present in the change, even if they are fighting fires in other areas of the organization.

Not High Enough in the Organization to Have Real Impact on Change

Sometimes the sponsor is not in the right position in the organization to drive the change. They may not have support from their leader. Or their priorities have realigned, and they no longer have influence on a high priority project. If this happens, you may want to connect with an additional leader to see if you can add a sponsor to the initiative. If it appears that the project timeline may be in jeopardy, advocate for your users to have the project paused, realigned, or re-baselined. It may make sense to change the date by which the project is expected to be completed.

Not Holding Directors, Managers, and Supervisors Responsible for Carrying the Message Forward

There are times when the sponsor doesn't hold their own downline or staff accountable for communicating the information about the change. When this occurs, the project team should request the problem be addressed with the sponsor at an executive level. An estimated 70 percent of projects fail due to lack of an active and visible sponsor. The risk is too high to ignore a lack of involvement.

Micromanaging Communication

Sponsors who want to be extremely involved in wordsmithing and developing communication can seem meddlesome to the team, but their interest in being involved is a good sign. However, micromanaging or reworking communication can sometimes add time into the schedule, resulting in delayed communications. If this is happening on your project, you may want to add an extra review week into the schedule. Be sure to alert the sponsor about their review and delivery dates.

Making Sponsor Meetings Matter

It's important to have frequent, productive meetings with your sponsor and a few members of the project team. This might seem basic, but I've attended many meetings without agendas or apparent purpose. As a change management leader, it is your responsibility to keep your sponsor constantly aware of the risks to and progress on the project. Having a specific agenda and expected outcomes keeps frustration at bay and promotes teamwork.

Frustration grows when meetings are unclear, lack agendas, or hold no one accountable for results. When there is a sense of accomplishment and a plan for moving progress forward, the sponsor and the team look forward to meetings, rather than dreading them.

READY-Set-Change Reflections

1. Do you feel confident and competent when working with organizational leaders?

2. Is your sponsor responsible for more than one change initiative? If so, do you know which is highest priority?

3. Are you engaging with the sponsor regularly? Do you have dedicated meeting time?

4. Do you see any obstacles or roadblocks impacting your sponsor? If so, how do you plan to address them?

Advance Communication and Advocacy

"Hey John!" Elizabeth called, "Can I talk with you a minute?"

John held the elevator door for Elizabeth.

"What's up?" he asked.

"Well, I'm working on advance communication for the Document Management Imaging System project. I've asked the technical and project teams if we can call the project the DMS – Document Management System – so we can create an engaging way to communicate about the project. Everyone said it's up to you," Elizabeth explained.

"I'm not exactly sure what that means," John replied, "but I'm in favor of getting something moving quickly. When people don't have enough time to absorb the message, we always have a problem. Since the clock is ticking, you're about to have a problem."

Elizabeth looked at the two other people in the elevator to see if they were listening to her conversation. "Well, I was thinking if we could use 'DMS,' it would tie into the EMR communication theme of learning to build and fly an airplane. You know how all airports have a three-letter code? Instead of ATL for Atlanta or LAX for Los Angeles, our destination will be DMS!" Elizabeth suddenly felt self-conscious as she realized everyone in the elevator was waiting for her to get off on her floor.

"I'm not a creative type. But if you have an idea of how to tie the two projects together, and you can get Allie and the EMR communication folks to agree, then it's fine by me," John paused, "but, you know I need to see a plan."

"Sure thing. Thanks!" Elizabeth shouted as she rushed to catch the closing elevator door and escape to her desk. She was relieved that she could now check with Allie and the communication group about her idea.

Allie listened to Elizabeth's account of her conversation with John. "Clear is better than clever," she replied.

"What?" asked Elizabeth.

"While I'm in favor of creative ideas, and I do like the 'destination DMS,' we need to make sure the message is clear and easy to *understand. With the help of the communications and marketing team we'll create a fun, clear, and memorable campaign. Then we can engage stakeholders and begin advance communication for the EMR system also."*

As Allie turned to her laptop to schedule a meeting, she added, "I'll set up some time for a small group of us to review your stakeholder assessment and create the communication plan. Our team just completed an inventory of all the communication tools available for the project. This inventory will apply to your project as well."

A combination of relief and excitement washed over Elizabeth. She'd have some help developing her plan, and communication could begin. The clock was ticking after all.

In its most recent *State of the Workplace* study, Gallup reported that people need to see and hear a message nine to sixteen times before they understand how the message applies to them.[7] Communication is essential for change initiatives, and people need time to recognize how they will be affected by the change. Leaders, project teams, and even sponsors often overestimate how effectively they are communicating. Users often report they feel surprised by change. Communication must start early. The process of transferring an idea is complex and creates opportunities for misunderstanding in both context and tone.

---

[7] Gallup, Inc, Gallup. "State of the American Workplace." Gallup.com, Gallup, 12 Dec. 2019, www.gallup.com/workplace/238085/state-american-workplace-report-2017.aspx

Context matters in communication. Each person's mental model creates context, meaning they may or may not receive communication the way you intended it. Sometimes even communication in the same location, but in different departments or units, can be contextually different. The tone or references need adjustment to ensure the message is received and shared across the organization effectively. Tone is the overall feeling or sentiment delivered through the language, context, or delivery method of the communication. Tone tends to be unit-specific and is sometimes hard to explain, but easily recognized when it's off.

There is much to consider when planning advance communication. Developing the message is an obvious step. Less obvious is the need to determine the medium, such as face-to-face, video, written, email blast, printed brochures, and posters. Finally, you must make decisions about timing for delivery.

A communication inventory can help determine which channels different stakeholders and end users use. For example, there may be a public facing magazine that's used to communicate with external stakeholders such as the general public, a specific electronic newsletter sent to managers in the organization, or a website for employees. All stakeholder groups and all communication channels must be included in the advance communication plan.

Because the sheer amount of communication tasks and audiences can become overwhelming, use a tool such as the READY-Set-Change Communication Plan to identify the messaging and strategy. Use the Communication Spreadsheet to schedule messages. Download this and other tools from the READY-Set-Change Model at

ReadySetChangeBook.com

The READY-Set-Change Communication Plan

How to Use the READY-Set-Change Communication Plan Spreadsheet

1. Capture the description of the change. Document the work completed in developing the Relevant and Relatable message. The description of the change and its associated benefits must be easy to understand. All the messages to different stakeholder groups should tie back to an overall theme.

2. Add stakeholders from the Stakeholder Identification and Assessment to the spreadsheet's "audience" column. You may add subgroups if needed.

3. Determine key messages, which are the main points you want your audience to hear and remember. You will have a number of key messages with different timing to address questions such as, "Why are we making this change? How will I be impacted? When will this affect me? What will success look like?" Use simple, non-technical language to tell the story of the change.

4. Identify the communication channels and vehicles you plan to use to deliver your key messages. There is no "one size fits all." Each stakeholder group will have multiple communication channels, some more effective than others. People typically need to hear a message between nine and sixteen times before recognizing that it impacts them.

5. Determine who creates communication, who it's from, as well as who delivers the message. Those who create the messages are not necessarily the best people to deliver them. For example, you may want to have the sponsor of the project deliver the

"why" messages, and then have the manager or supervisor reiterate the "why" and add the "how" messages. People are more likely be receptive to information from their direct supervisors than from other sources.

6. The communication plan should also include a schedule of when the various communications will be delivered. The schedule should include draft dates, reviews, and final delivery dates.

As with many of the tools, the Advance Communication Plan is never really finished. It's constantly evolving.

Watch for "Just Send an Email" Thinking

As a consultant, I worked with a large government agency to replace an old mainframe system with modern technology to handle financial transactions. This is a common type of project in large organizations. Archaic systems have reached the end of their support lifespans or are so expensive to keep patching together, that it's fiscally smarter and technically easier to replace them.

On projects such as this, the project team begins work months, or even years, before the employees will see or experience the new system. The project team is immersed in the project and may not recognize that no one outside of the team knows what is happening. When the project team nears the finish line for their work, , they might assume that the employees, end users, and stakeholders are prepared and ready to implement as well.

In this project, the leaders figured they could "just send an email" to let stakeholders and users know the system was ready to use.

> *Few employees were aware of the coming change, but almost everyone used the system for submitting travel expenses and payroll. Immediate action was needed to avoid the chaos that was about to unfold.*
>
> *The first step was to let everyone know about the change, with a specific message from the agency director. This required much more than simply sending an email.*
>
> *A robust website was created to specifically focus on helping employees get ready for the new system. It featured an excel document called a crosswalk table, where you could enter the code you previously used and the new code you needed would be highlighted.*
>
> *The agency developed posters and brochures to hang near the elevators. Leaders conducted webinars and face-to-face town hall meetings to get the word out about this change. Despite getting a late start on communication, the website, posters and webinars were well received and extremely helpful to the stakeholders and users. Videos and a travelling support "pop-up lab" sealed the deal on helping users adopt the change.*

When you hear "just send an email," you must advocate for your end users and stakeholders. They deserve more than an email to notify them that things in their world will be very different very soon.

With the plan in place, you can create sample messages and tools for the stakeholder groups. I like to start developing content as Frequently Asked Questions (FAQ) section for the webpage. Work with subject matter experts to identify answers to questions about functionality, timing, benefits, and training. Once you have all the facts, it's easier to create communication materials for the change.

Capture information regularly and direct people to the site often. This will encourage them to make it a habit to check the site, where communication is always accessible. Share the site in presentations and written communication, and direct stakeholders to your site for information and updates. This will train stakeholders to be self-sufficient, because they'll know where to go to find current information.

When I'm developing a web page or site I include:

- A paragraph about the project to explain the benefits of the change. It should be short and simple, without jargon
- Information about training. Most people will first experience the impact of the change through training. No need to post the training plan, but provide links to online training, directions on how to sign up or where to go, and links to new training resources (such as job aids, videos, and guides) as they become available.
- Communication tools, such as flyers or posters, that people can print for their units or departments
- Videos about benefits, real users, and project updates

Continuing to ask, "How will this impact stakeholders?" or "How is it going to affect end users?" might make you feel like a broken record. But the job of finding out what will impact the end user is the role of the change management professional. It's like being a translator, explaining technical jargon into "kitchen English." Think of yourself as an end-user detective, whose job it is to figure out who needs what type of information about the change.

Keep in mind that it's hard to over communicate with stakeholders and end users about something that will have a major impact on them. The goals is to break through the day-to-day noise of work to ensure that everyone is aware of and preparing for change.

"I'm so relieved!" Elizabeth exclaimed as she reviewed her notes. She was creating a list of the messages she would send to various stakeholder groups. The communication inventory that the EMR team had created was comprehensive. After listing stakeholders, she was going to assign owners, reviewers, and dates for every communication.

She felt somewhat organized after meeting with the team. "I thought I'd never have a handle on the messages and documents we need or know when to send them and who to send to. Now I see the flow and can begin to develop our messaging."

Allie nodded in agreement. "Yes, it's helpful to see all of the pieces laid out. But remember the communication plan is very fluid. You'll have a lot of changes along the way, particularly in your advocacy role."

"I'm still not sure that I understand the advocate role," Elizabeth confessed.

Allie nodded her head and started to draw on the back of her agenda. "It's a little confusing," she agreed, "but let's see if I can clarify. Advocacy works in two directions. In one direction, you and others on the team, such as project managers, sponsors, and leaders, must advocate for and promote the change in a visible and active way. Advocating for the change means that you support the team. Even if you are tired or frustrated by the change, you speak positively to others about this change."

"You mean, don't come in and complain that the change is taking too long, or is difficult?" Elizabeth asked.

"Yes," Allie replied. "You must keep moving forward and promoting the change to team members, stakeholders, end users, and anyone else impacted. At the same time, I know you don't want to just provide 'happy talk' that everything is great when it may not be. Acknowledging losses and difficulty is the caring thing to do, and it helps people move through change. We don't want to get stuck in the transition, though., So, even when you're recognizing frustrations, you must also remind everyone of the benefit of the change."

"Hey," Jake stuck his head in the meeting room and pointed at Elizabeth. "See you downstairs at five o'clock? We're getting behind on our training for the race!"

"Is that all you think about?" Elizabeth sighed. "I'm tired of running, and I've already run a 10K in our training runs. Can't we take a break?"

Allie looked expectantly at Jake.

"The answer," he paused, "is no. See you at five." He shut the door.

"See," said Allie, "Jake knows how to advocate for your goal. He knows you're tired of training, but he's not going to stop pushing so that you can both achieve your goal."

Elizabeth rolled her eyes. *"I see you're advocating for Jake,"* she teased.

"Fair enough," laughed Allie. *"The other responsibility of advocacy is to be a representative for your stakeholders. When you attend meetings or see progress reports, you might notice that something essential to the stakeholders may be delayed or not delivered. If that happens, you must voice your concerns and explain to the project, technical, or leadership team why it matters to stakeholders."*

"You know I don't like conflict," said Elizabeth. *"Are you saying that I should argue with the leaders or technical team?"*

Allie shook her head. *"Not argue, just advocate. For example, let's say the technical team discovers they can't complete an interface they plan to provide, which will cause the end users to add a manual process in their workflow. You remember Jake's example with the donut shop?"*

Elizabeth nodded her head. *"They had to use two systems, one paper and one online, because they didn't have a way to keep the counter and drive-thru orders in one system. Are you saying the users needed an advocate to explain why having these two systems was going to be a disaster?"* Elizabeth asked.

"Maybe if they could see Jake's frustration, multiplied by hundreds of customers, they'd have figured out a different solution, or would've taken more time to get it right," Allie prompted.

"But how do we know that someone didn't try to advocate for them?" Elizabeth asked.

"Well," said Allie, "we don't know. But do you think when they implemented this ordering system, they meant to create a manual intervention and snafu for all of their stores? I'm sure they didn't intend for that to happen." Allie paused. "I don't mean to sound negative, but identifying impact is tricky for those of us in change management. You see, if I do a great job of getting people ready for change, eliminate potential issues, and provide users with what they need to adopt the change, we don't hear complaints or frustrations from users. The lack of noise and frustration means I did a great job."

"Wait," said Elizabeth, "are you telling me the only way my boss will know if I did a good job getting everyone ready for the new system is if he doesn't hear anything?"

"Much of what we do is preventative." Allie continued, "We're preventing problems and issues through preparation. Think about it. When you exercise, eat well, and take care of yourself, you're less likely to get sick. That's preventative. Or if you service your furnace, have the roof inspected, and keep your downspouts clear, you may avoid emergencies with your house. No one pays much attention to what doesn't happen, and much of our work is like that too. So, when we have the chance to advocate for our stakeholders and end users, we must do so. The adage that 'an ounce of prevention is worth a pound of cure' is especially true when it comes to advocacy." Allie paused to check Elizabeth's understanding.

"So, don't be a jerk, and don't be afraid to raise an issue on behalf of stakeholders and end users," Elizabeth summarized.

"And customers like Jake," Allie reminded.

"Shoot!" Elizabeth jumped as she glanced at her phone. "Speaking of Jake, I'm due in the parking lot. Thanks a lot, Allie!"

Advocacy is two-sided when it comes to leading change. One side is an understanding or expectation of those involved with the change. Organization leaders, project team members, business owners, and subject matter experts are advocating for and supporting the change. Advocates speak positively about change and look for ways to help others become engaged in and enthusiastic about the change. This requires a positive mindset and the ability to put aside the day-to-day struggles of the project work to focus on the positive benefits that are to come. Some people will find this difficult. It's helpful to engage those who really struggle with promoting the change to ensure their questions are answered and that they have the information they need to feel comfortable.

The second side of advocacy is more specifically involved with the change itself. This type of advocacy involves looking for issues and problems that might affect end users and stakeholders, and then escalating those concerns to project leadership for investigation.

Sometimes I find these issues and problems when I'm doing stakeholder assessments. It's not uncommon to hear about a work process that hadn't been identified in other discussions, or about a special report not disclosed to the technical team. If I'm not sure it's been considered or discovered by the technical team, I inquire about a potential impact on the project.

Communicating with the project or technical team to see if others are aware of and planning for this issue is one of the roles of a change leader. When an issue is discovered, change leaders must be diligent in escalating issues through the appropriate structures on a project.

Getting Your Team's Attention

You may find yourself working on an issue that will cause disruption and distress to end users. If it seems like you can't get attention on resolving the problem, you'll need to engage sponsors and organizational leaders. Describe steps you've already taken with the project team and technical team to have this issue recognized. Don't be afraid to ask for help.

*A word of warning!

Be honest about whether the issue will affect users and stakeholders in a significant way or will cause harm. Sometimes business owners or subject matter experts can use your advocacy to get something that has already been deemed out of scope. This is where the politics of the change and the project come into play. Sometimes business owners are unhappy and want additional functionality that has already been determined by the leadership team or sponsor to be out of scope or unachievable in this project. The business may sometimes raise this additional work as an issue for the end users, and then lobby for additional scope. Sometimes, they will engage the change leader to fight on behalf of the end users for these extra features.

This doesn't happen often, but it bears keeping in mind. The potential misuse of advocates is one of the many reasons why the change leader should have regular meetings with the project manager and have a seat on the project team.

When you focus on readiness, make sure there's clear communication across all areas. Provide opportunities for open discussion and regular meetings where issues can be easily raised. The adoption of the technology and acceptance of change requires consistent focus on what is best for stakeholders and end users.

Speaking Up

Advocacy means raising your voice when something seems wrong.

I was brought onto a project quite late, just three months from go-live. A new system would enable the staff at physicians' offices to bill the state for health care they'd provided to qualified beneficiaries, and to enter immunization records directly into the system. Under the old process, the physicians' offices would fax immunization records for someone at the state to enter manually.

As we reviewed the schedule for this initiative, it became clear the physicians and their staff were going to be forced to adopt the new immunization system in three months. No one had communicated with the physicians' offices that this change was on the way! The schedule also showed these offices would start using the new system for a different function many months later.

In my role as an advocate, I raised concerns about physicians and their staff having to log in and use this system for immunizations, while also using their existing system for billing. They would have to use two systems to do the work they currently did with just one. The plan would require the physicians' staff to train for the new system twice: once, in three months for immunization records, and then again, many months later, for billing. The technical timeline was driving all decisions about the schedule.

As the change leader, I worked with the team to create a user-centric map showing all the stakeholders and end users. We then added how they would be using the system, and whether they would be using it for one process or multiple processes.

We clarified our goal and made a decision to have just one launch per user group, grouping similar users to go live together. With this new focus, the schedule was rebuilt. The technical team could finish their development according to the original schedule, but users would only adopt the system when all the components they needed to do their work had been completed. This revision altered the planned rollout and contributed to a successful adoption of the change.

This is the kind of advocacy necessary for our stakeholders and users to have a chance at full adoption. Many times, the project and technical team can't see the impact on the end users and stakeholders. It's up to those who are leading readiness to understand how the end user will be affected, and then share this essential information with the rest of the team.

READY-Set-Change Reflections

1. Have you captured all types of communication vehicles in a communication inventory?

2. How can you coordinate sending messages through with the corporate communication team?

3. Does your sponsor recognize your advocacy role? Will they support advocacy for stakeholders and end users?

4. How will you alert your sponsor to develop support if you need to escalate an issue?

Develop Support and Ensure Readiness with Training

Jake slowly repeated John's words to make sure he had heard him clearly. "We can't provide the level of support we've indicated is necessary in the plan?"

John nodded, "Not unless you can show the CIO how the support plan will pay for itself. We aren't going to have the budget. Sorry."

Jake was frustrated as he went to meet with Elizabeth and Allie. He was hesitant to share this news. When he repeated John's warning, Elizabeth got quiet. But Allie jumped to her feet and started writing on the white board.

"Okay, not a big deal," she said to Jake and Elizabeth's surprise. *"Let's multiply the number of physicians impacted by their average hourly rate. Do you think $300 per hour will do?"*

Elizabeth stared at the number on the board and nodded. She wasn't sure what Allie was working on.

"Then with a thousand physicians, one hour of downtime will cost approximately $300,000 in terms of impact." Allie was picking up speed, *"How about the physician's office staff? The hourly rate is not as high, but there are more of them. So if there are three support staff to one physician, we are looking at approximately $150,000 an hour, right?"*

"I'm not following," Elizabeth said.

Allie paused and looked at Jake, *"Okay, it's hard to justify your budget because it is preventative. So we need to show how the support plan will save time, money, and negativity. To explain the importance of providing this level of support we must show how much an hour or two of struggle and delay will cost. If each of our one thousand physicians is non-productive because of the new system, that will cost us $300,000 dollars an hour. What if they are non-productive for five hours in a month due to lack of support?"*

"Then we get into serious money." Jake was already starting a spreadsheet to track all the costs identified.

"What if their staff doesn't know how to find the information needed for the physician? Or if they miss billing something because it's not

indexed correctly? Or worse, the lack of support for staff makes it difficult for the physician to take care of their patients?" Elizabeth *suggested.*

"Now we are looking at harm on top of cost," said Allie. *"The money we spend in support is minor compared to the cost of going live without full support."*

Jake looked at Elizabeth, "You have access to the salaries and rates of everyone who works here. Do you think we could put together a financial case for supporting the doctors and their staff?"

"Yes, and I think that our risk management group would like to chime in as well. They do this type of calculation frequently." Elizabeth *was feeling hopeful.*

"Great!" Allie erased her calculations. "Let's set up a meeting with John and lay out the financial case for this level of support. Development is key to successful implementation and sustaining change. We plan on having a superuser group in place, reviewing and updating training materials continually, and having a robust help desk. All these factors have a huge impact when it comes to adopting change. Once we show the financial case for support, we might have a good shot at making it happen."

The development of a robust support plan, in addition to training and development of new skills, is key to a prepared and ready team. Gallup's *State of the Workplace* poll provides evidence that developing people makes a huge difference in knowledge and confidence, which helps individuals feel ready for change.[8] Implementation of technology creates a critical need for training and development, so people to know how to use the system and how to adapt their workflows and processes.

Support is where you can get the most bang for your buck. Support encompasses the help desk, job aids, updates, labs, one-on-one mentoring and coaching, meals, sympathy, and troubleshooting. There are many ways to provide support.

User Acceptance Testing

User acceptance testing (UAT) generally happens three to six months before go-live. This is when actual users of the system try using it and determine if the system is working as anticipated, and, as the name suggests, whether users will accept it. The training team should work closely with the UAT team to use some test scripts for training scenarios. User acceptance testing participants should also review training documents.

Superusers

Creating an embedded team, culled from the training team, UAT testers, or help desk staff to assist with challenges and work with the project team to share new information. This team is usually called

---

[8] Gallup, Inc, Gallup. "State of the American Workplace." Gallup.com, Gallup, 12 Dec. 2019, www.gallup.com/workplace/238085/state-american-workplace-report-2017.aspx

Superusers or Power Users. They're essential when it comes to onsite support for work groups.

Superusers have a unique role and skill set because of their involvement in the project. They will need extra system training and possibly expanded access in the system to help troubleshoot issues. The change or project team should meet regularly with Superusers to provide updates they can share with their respective work units. When someone in the unit is having difficulty, the Superuser is there to assist with identifying issues for help desk calls or problem tickets. Superusers' training should begin before general user training. Superusers should recognize that they must stay in the role for six to nine months after the system goes live.

In addition to system training, superusers will benefit from additional training on coaching, logging issues, listening, and advocacy. Superusers should also receive recognition and rewards for the important role they play. Many superuser groups stay intact for a year or more as the system continues to evolve. Superusers are excellent resources to help keep training up to date, support the help desk, and onboard new team members.

Training

The goal of training is to ensure end users have the skills they need to do their jobs when the change is implemented. Creating meaningful training is a highly developed skill. Having spent many years creating and delivering training, I can say that it is worthy of its own book. So I won't go into great detail about how to develop training here. Development of training requires deep consideration of complex issues, such as which area "owns" training, how training will be delivered, what will be taught, and how you'll know if you got it right.

Many technology vendors include training as part of the project and provide materials to use. This is a relief to most project teams. However, the type of training the vendor provides as a part of their contract is usually not what the end users need. Sometimes the technology vendor will provide training materials for the system itself, but not necessarily for how people will use the system. Vendor training tends to focus on showing, for example, the type of information that can be entered in each field of the software. After more than two decades of technology system implementations, I can honestly say I have never seen vendor training that could be used as-is for stakeholders or end users.

When developing training, consideration should begin with the stakeholder identification and assessment, and discovering how people's jobs will be different. Then training should be based on the role, rather than on the way the software works. Those who will be doing their jobs with the new system need to be involved in both user acceptance testing and discussions about training.

Developing training requires work with subject matter experts to review each job role and determine:

◇ Does this role need to do something differently than what they're currently doing?
◇ Is this a skill that can be taught?
◇ How can this skill be taught?
◇ Does this skill apply to other roles?

With this understanding of what is needed, begin creating a curriculum path for each job role. The result is a curriculum map, which provides a view of all the courses you plan to offer, who should take each course, and the sequence of the training courses. Developing a curriculum map is one goal of the training plan.

In addition to a curriculum map, encourage a focus on great training. Instructors should be engaging presenters who can make technical material interesting. Someone reading PowerPoint slides or clicking on system fields while narrating is not going to cut it. Great training can be online or onsite, but never boring or confusing.

The training curriculum should be designed for different levels of users. Those who will look up information or do basic queries are level one. Users who work daily in the system need level two training. Level three is reserved for specialists who need in-depth and advanced training.

Training really must be hands-on so that users and stakeholders can practice both physically and mentally. The goal is to give people the ability to do their jobs with the new tool, rather than becoming experts in the tool. There are many models for delivering training. On technology projects, you'll usually use a specific copy of the software as a training environment. The training environment will have "staged" test data for stepping through scenarios during training sessions. Creating and populating a training environment is a specialized skill. Work with an experienced training manager or environment creation to get this right. Once the training environment is created, you can use it for hands-on training or as a practice environment or sandbox leading up to go-live. After launch, the environment can be repurposed to facilitate help desk research, troubleshooting, ongoing support sessions.

Many implementations use Just-In-Time (JIT) training, which is delivered in a short time window, right before go-live, so the information is fresh in the minds of end users. Depending on the number of employees needing training, it can be difficult to ramp up enough classrooms and instructors to provide JIT training to everyone.

The PO Dance

On a large financial system replacement project, we had a complex set of software screens for procurement. To complete the purchase order, you had to complete the information on three screens, save and then go back to the first screen, add information, jump over to the fourth screen, check a box, and then go back to the third screen to save again and submit.

All the forward and backward motion felt like a dance to me, going first in one direction and then in another – "One, Two, Cha-cha-cha, Three, Four, Cha-cha-cha." To help our users remember the sequence, we created a mouse pad with a dance step footprints diagram on it (old school like Arthur Miller), and we called it the "PO Dance."

The PO Dance helped our end users remember the steps they needed to create purchase orders in the new system. And it did so in a fun, easy way.

Training Logistics

When rolling out training, logistics can make or break you. For hands-on training, you'll need to have computers available in classrooms. For online training or awareness training, webinars and video-conference calls can be effective. Learning management systems are excellent delivery tools for online training. Measuring and evaluating training helps us determine if the training is effective. We can also measure whether the participants can perform tasks or answer questions that were taught in the training.

Again, a caveat that this work is never "done." There will always be more information, new functionality, and of course, software updates and new employees.

Developing, conducting, and evaluating training requires specialized skills. Even if an organization does not have dedicated change management resources, they generally have a training team. This training team can assess the training needs, design and develop training to meet those needs, and implement and evaluate the training. Leverage those resources in your organization; collaborate to determine how the training and information from the evaluations can be used to help the users adopt the change more quickly. Doing so can help you realize the benefits of the change sooner.

Pre-Go-live Meeting

Before going live, organize a mandatory readiness meeting with all the business areas, technical team, project team, sponsors, and executives. During this meeting, each business owner reviews status and must agree to move forward with the change.

This is a great time for additional questions to be asked and for clarifications to be made. I've been a part of such meetings both in person and remotely. Formats range from simply reviewing a checklist to conducting a complete walk-through. The goal is to resolve any questions and come to agreement on how to proceed with the rollout of the project.

Go-live Support

When a system goes live, the project team is usually elated! They feel that they have "made it" and are understandably relieved and exhausted. For the users in the business, however, the challenge has just begun.

Now the people who have been worried, training, or ignoring the change have nowhere to hide. They have work to do and must figure out how to do their work in this new world of the "future state." Hopefully, they have the knowledge and understanding they need to survive and thrive. But even with the best plans and good intentions, something can still go wrong. If this happens, the project team should quickly communicate with the business to provide additional information, offer training, or assist where needed.

Even though support at go-live is usually planned, post-launch support is sometimes an afterthought. An assumption is often made that the help desk will be able to assist with all support issues. What I've discovered, however, is that the training team is the best support for both the go-live and post go-live periods. The training team is usually composed of people who, after training for several weeks, really know the system. They are great communicators and practiced at providing instruction. The most effective option is to offer a go-live support team that has a combination of help desk and training team members. An open video conference line and remote desktop support can provide global support. There is also great value in personal, one-on-one assistance at various locations. The productivity rescue of a good go-live support team is well worth the expense. Beyond the immediate financial benefits, the hope and guidance that they provide employees decreases negativity, stress, and lost productivity. The US Bureau of Labor statistics estimates these hidden costs add up to $500 billion each year.

Pop-Up Labs Save the Day

On a project implementing a new state financial system. there was a state-wide approach to training and change. The scale of the change for nearly 50,000 employees was so large that the vendor decided to provide some videos for training and call it a day. One of the larger agencies decided to invest in their own change management and training teams, with support from our change management consulting firm. We collaborated with the procurement team to create training for those who worked in the procurement area. We also developed a number of job aids for the reimbursement of travel expenses. While we were aware that the implementation would be difficult, the issues with the travel expense reimbursement system were unmanageable.

Our agency had nearly 15,000 employees who routinely travelled to and from multiple client sites per day, all paying for their expenses out-of-pocket and relying on reimbursement. The

---

frustration and aggravation of trying to use the new system reached a fevered pitch. Leadership became aware of the stress the change was creating. They approved a special post go-live onsite support team to conduct "pop-up labs" at some of the 120 remote offices.

These pop-up labs were structured as mobile training centers with laptops, three trainers, and a scheduling coordinator. Employees in remote offices could book 45-minute, one-on-one appointments with one of the trainers. Together, employees and trainers would work through the system, submitting the travel expenses so employees could be paid. The cost for the pop-up lab was not insignificant, but the payoff was enormous! This strategy helped to manage the negativity and frustration that had been building. The pop-up lab team was able to provide direct feedback to the travel department and the project team. This feedback led to system improvements that made it easier for users to submit expenses. The pop-up lab team provided essential go-live support for the project.

READY-Set-Change Reflections

1. Do you have a plan for ongoing or individual support post go-live?

2. Have you identified team members who can create additional training materials, job aids, crosswalks and guides as needed?

3. Do you have capability to provide support through remote access or video conference with users?

4. How do you plan to collect ideas for support from users?

"Why" Is the Answer to Resistance

"I don't think you should be spending your time helping Elizabeth with the DMIS project." Tom was the Chief Human Resource Officer, so Allie was confused by his statement. After all, he was the one who'd had assigned Elizabeth to lead this change. Allie assumed he'd want Elizabeth to be successful.

"Why would you think that?" Allie responded. "I'm helping Elizabeth because this will help our EMR project. The goodwill we develop from a successful rollout of this project will be a vital asset as we begin a more difficult implementation for physicians and staff," Allie lobbied.

"Well, it seems to me we're wasting money. I haven't heard anything about the project in a while, except for the fact that you have a big plan for supporting the physicians and staff. I don't think we need to provide so much support for the physicians and their teams. It's expensive," countered Tom.

Allie was quiet. After a moment, she thanked Tom for his input and went in search of John, the PMO Director.

What did it mean that the CHRO was questioning the approach and the plan they'd been developing? Why was he opposed to her helping Elizabeth? It seemed like he was trying to sabotage the plan.

Allie stopped in her tracks. She suddenly realized she was seeing resistance in one of its sneakiest forms.

Resistance was showing up as the concerned leader who voices support for the plan in public, but soon begins to speak negatively about the project to others. She had seen leaders end support prematurely or focus on costs rather than on the savings and benefits of support. Meeting with Tom was frustrating, and Allie knew it was time to consider where resistance might be appearing from different stakeholders involved in the project.

Allie then realized she hadn't shared with Elizabeth the types of resistance she might encounter as they implemented the change. She wanted to help Elizabeth recognize how to reduce resistance before it was too late.

"Why are we doing this?" is not a question you can answer just once. "Why" must be answered in multiple ways and multiple times. You must be able to articulate the "why" every time you communicate. There is a deep human need to understand. If we don't honor the need to understand the why, people may not make the change and fail to adopt.

Change resistance is often seen as stubbornness or a refusal to move forward with the change, but that might not always be the case. What if what is perceived as resistance is natural skepticism or caution?

There are generally four types of responses to readiness efforts. While not all individuals will fit neatly into a single type, most of the resistance you will encounter will show up in one of these ways.

Commander or Fighter

Commanders are natural leaders. They are those to whom others when they are uncertain about the direction to take. Commanders work hard to visibly champion and lead the movement toward change. The Commander will move forward on an idea even without having all the details on a project, which is extremely valuable for leadership. Commanders are open to change; they enjoy being leaders and exploring new worlds. If the Commander is always kept informed, they are excellent leaders.

The default resistance mode for a Commander is Fighter. When a Commander is not kept informed, or feels like they've been misled or undervalued, they become Fighters, leading the charge against the change. When the Commander doesn't buy in, watch out! The Fighter will emerge in a visible and vocal way against what they believe is bad judgement. Fighters have the leadership skills to rally against change. They are direct about what they see and aren't worried about political ramifications or about being seen as unsupportive. They rely on data and their gut in determining if something is worth supporting.

Strategy for Fighter Resistance

To deal with a Fighter, provide a lot of data and follow-up discussion. Give them an opportunity to state their arguments and objections. If they feel they are being placated or appeased, they are quick to jump on their horse and lead the charge against the change. Keep the Fighter at bay with accurate data, discussion, and involvement in choosing direction. Provide information quickly, and keep them updated on a weekly or daily basis.

Socializer or Saboteur

Socializers have excellent networks and use their contacts to increase enthusiasm about ideas they understand and support. Getting a Socializer on board early is one way to increase acceptance and readiness for an initiative. The Socializer seems to know everyone in the organization. They can provide great insight to both the project team and stakeholders about who'll be impacted. Socializers are great in communication roles. They are not necessarily the people to look to when you need a decision. But to publicize the decision, there's no one better.

However, when the Socializer doesn't believe in or support the change you may have trouble ahead. The same social skills that help communicate, socialize, and gain acceptance can also be used to sabotage the change. Saboteurs are skilled when it comes to spreading negative information. They may begin sharing about the status of the project and veer off into their opinion of why it won't work. They take on a role as an "insider" sharing with others. Saboteurs are difficult to root out because they are spreading negative perceptions in a whisper campaign or with sarcastic delivery. Lack of access to and communication with the project is what the Socializer/Saboteur fears.

Strategy for Saboteur Resistance

If you believe the Socializer has become a Saboteur, you must cut them off from meetings, briefings, and other communication. Let the stakeholders know the Saboteur is no longer involved in the project. Assign team accountability for communication to ensure messaging stays positive and distributed among a number of individuals.

Understander or Underminer

The Understander needs a deep understanding of the change. Many people in organizations are happy to support what they understand. Spend time to assist the Understander by reviewing the importance of the change, the story of the change. and the anticipated outcomes of the change. You'll be rewarded with an ardent supporter who is consistently supportive of change. The Understander is often the person to whom others turn when they are frustrated about a change. Preparing Understanders with tools and strategies to explain the change to others is an important task. Those who like stability and structure, and who value a systematic approach to change, are important in their roles as Understanders. This group is very people-focused. Unlike the Socializers, who want to be out front sharing the news of the project, Understanders want to keep people engaged while exploring the new way of working.

If the Understander doesn't have the information they need to thoroughly understand the change, they may become an Underminer. Underminers damage the initiative by telling others they don't know why the change is happening and that they don't support the change. They may be quiet and fail to develop support or a readiness response to the change. Undermining is difficult to see. It is often communicated through a rolling of the eyes, a sarcastic comment, and a wait-and-see attitude that can persuade others to resist readiness.

Strategy for Underminer Resistance

If your Understander has started to undermine the change, you must involve them in project work. Ask them to attend meetings, develop communication, or direct some type of team event. In other words, help Underminers focus on people rather than on technology. Assigning Underminers to plan team events may seem counterintuitive. But partnering them with a Socializer to do so is often the best way to move them back to understanding.

Detailer or Derailer

The Detailer needs details about the change: how it will affect them, how it will be implemented, all the tiny details that may not even be settled. The more details, the better for the Detailer. Detailers will analyze and point out gaps in the plan or vague assumptions that increase risk in the initiative. The Detailer needs a lot of information and will not support the change without detail and analysis. They want to know with nearly 100 percent assurance this is the right move or decision to make. Their natural tendency is to resist change until they have enough data or information to reconcile themselves to changing direction.

Sometimes Detailers develop "analysis paralysis," where decisions are held up in the desire for more data. Provide Detailers with enough data to make them comfortable, and they may be your greatest supporters. The Detailer needs time to absorb information and values making a thoughtful, well-informed decision. No matter how much time it takes, they will not be rushed. If your sponsor is a Detailer, schedule more time and enough detail for decisions.

When Detailers don't have enough information or feel rushed, they may become Derailers. Derailers delay, avoid, or fail to provide support for the project. Derailing can appear as challenging comments, development of shadow systems, actively telling others how to work around the new technology, or speaking poorly about the initiative. Derailers can be effective in distracting the organization by adding requirements to the project or refusing to support or make decisions. The best way to deal with a Derailer is not to create one in the first place. This means you must provide the Detailer with the information they need to keep the entire change on track. If you have a sponsor that's a Derailer, you may need to request assistance from leadership for guidance or even a new sponsor.

Strategy for Derailer Resistance
There is no such thing as too much data for the Detailer. Schedule meetings and provide agendas in advance. Ask how they like to

receive information. Share information as soon as you can, and provide an organized, comprehensive list of project goals. Derailers often have insight about project impacts, and they need time to develop a response to questions or issues raised. Provide weekly feedback to Derailers about project progress. Ask for their recommendations to help them engage and contribute.

READY-Set-Change Reflections

1. Have you incorporated your "why" into communication for each stakeholder or user group?

2. Do you see resistance occurring in a particular area of the business?

3. Is the sponsor able to address resistance that may be appearing in the organization?

	Commander / Fighter	**Socializer / Saboteur**
Strength:	Leader promotes and supports change	Social Connector promotes and gains social acceptance of the change
Resistance Mode:	Actively speaks against the change	Subtly sabotages change through sarcasm and/or negative comments
Make sure to..	Keep Commanders updated with information about the change and stories about progress.	Keep socializers engaged by inviting them to meetings, events and activities. Ask for their help in with communication.
Examples	**John**, the PMO Director. is a Commander and communicates the change to the organization even without the plan detail.	**Jake,** the Project Manager, has a lot of friends and connections. He actively speaks well of the change. **Allie,** the Change Management Consultant, is outgoing and makes a point to visit with many leaders throughout the organization and keep them updated about change.

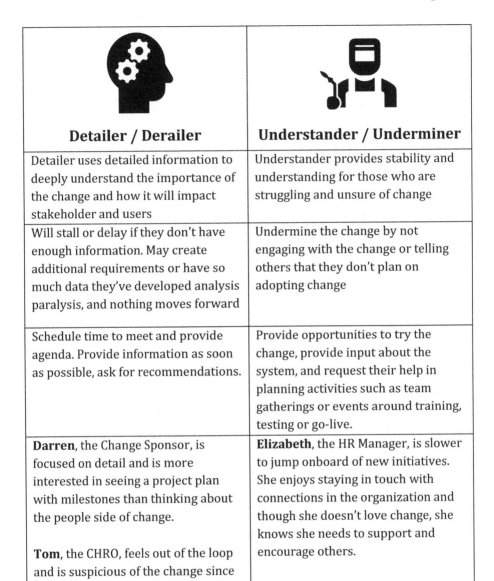

Detailer / Derailer	Understander / Underminer
Detailer uses detailed information to deeply understand the importance of the change and how it will impact stakeholder and users	Understander provides stability and understanding for those who are struggling and unsure of change
Will stall or delay if they don't have enough information. May create additional requirements or have so much data they've developed analysis paralysis, and nothing moves forward	Undermine the change by not engaging with the change or telling others that they don't plan on adopting change
Schedule time to meet and provide agenda. Provide information as soon as possible, ask for recommendations.	Provide opportunities to try the change, provide input about the system, and request their help in planning activities such as team gatherings or events around training, testing or go-live.
Darren, the Change Sponsor, is focused on detail and is more interested in seeing a project plan with milestones than thinking about the people side of change. **Tom**, the CHRO, feels out of the loop and is suspicious of the change since he hears just a bit of information here and there.	**Elizabeth**, the HR Manager, is slower to jump onboard of new initiatives. She enjoys staying in touch with connections in the organization and though she doesn't love change, she knows she needs to support and encourage others.

READY, Set, Change!

009

Dress Rehearsal

"I'm nervous" Elizabeth admitted.

Jake nodded and continued pinning her race bib on her back. "I know, but this is a great rehearsal for you. I'll be waiting at the finish line. I wish I could run with you, but my hamstring is just starting to heal, and I don't want to it to flare up."

Elizabeth had agreed to run a 10K with Jake as a practice for their upcoming race. Now that she was running it alone, she was anxious.

"Look, the goal is the same," Jake counseled. "This rehearsal will help us figure out if there's a problem we didn't anticipate or if you need to make any changes. You'll do great!"

She gave Jake a thumbs-up and lined up with a couple of women who looked a bit nervous as well. When the starting horn sounded, Elizabeth began to run. She felt clumsy. She couldn't seem to get her stride with so many people crowding her. As the runners started to spread out, though, she began to feel more comfortable. At the 5K mark, she tried to increase her speed. Suddenly she was uncomfortable. Her right sock was bunching up and rubbing the ball of her foot, which was making her hobble. She wasn't sure if she should stop and adjust it or just keep going.

"I guess that's the point of rehearsal," Elizbeth told herself as she stopped to adjust her sock and tie her shoe. She figured avoiding a blister was better than making great time.

"Smart choice," Jake commented at the finish, handing her a bottle of water. "Getting a blister this close to our big race would've been a problem, and your time wasn't impacted that much."

Elizabeth was both relieved and proud of herself for finishing her first race. "This was a great idea Jake," she admitted. "Now I feel like I'm really ready for our Haborside race. I'm taking tomorrow off, though!"

"Understandable," Jake agreed.

Reflecting on her race as she drove home, she thought of Jake calling the race a rehearsal. Elizabeth thought about the plays she had done in high school. She'd performed in almost every production.

To get ready for the show, they'd rehearse sections of the play each night for a month. The week before the show, they rehearsed the entire *play each night. Dress rehearsal took place the day before opening night and was always exciting. Putting on the costumes and make-up, and using props, lighting, and sound effects just as they would in performance made it all real. There were always adjustments to make: a misplaced prop so the actor couldn't get to it during a scene, light cues missed, or make-up that aged someone too much, or not enough.*

The 10K race was a dress rehearsal. Her 'costume,' the shoe and sock, had needed adjustment, and now she knew she'd have to figure out a better sock/shoe combination for her half marathon. She finally felt ready for the Harborside race with Jake.

"I'm going to figure out how we can have a 'dress rehearsal' for my project," Elizabeth told Allie on Monday.

"That's a great idea," encouraged Allie. "I think you're on to something."

"It might seem strange but if we rehearse how the physicians' offices will scan and index the different documents they get from patients, from other providers, and forms used in the office, we'll know if we've forgotten something. I'm going to create some scripts that each office can use to perform their dress rehearsal. That will help identify miscues and confusion with either process or technology." Elizabeth was excited about this idea for the physicians and their staff.

Just then her phone buzzed, and she recognized the number of her youngest son's school. He was sick and needed to go home. Elizabeth reflexively started to call her husband, but remembered he'd moved 45 minutes away now that they'd separated. A wave of anxiety and unexpected sadness hit her. She could feel her eyes burning with tears and Allie watching her.

"Allie, could you attend the project team meeting for me? I need to pick up my son from school."

"Yes, I'm attending anyway. Hope he feels better," Allie offered as she headed out.

"Well, I guess this is my dress rehearsal for being a single parent," Elizabeth mused on her drive to school. "Today I can work remotely, but not always. I need to figure out who can help me with childcare when I can't leave work for sick kids or school vacations. I'm not sure who to trust, or if someone could come to our house, but I need a plan."

As she pulled into the school parking lot, Elizabeth was both grateful for the chance to pick up her son and very aware an adjustment was needed to keep her "on stage" at work.

Dress rehearsal provides the opportunity to practice with process, roles, and technology. It can uncover decisions that haven't been made or processes that are still undefined.

Planning and implementing a formal dress rehearsal process promotes readiness.Reading an account of how to do something is different than being truly ready to do it. It's common for organizations to practice readiness. It's why we conduct fire drills to practice the action we'd take in case of a fire, or tornado drills to practice where to shelter and what to do.

Ceremony is a part of readiness. Marking graduation from high school or university with a ceremony, putting on a cap and gown, receiving diplomas and congratulations marks the change from student to graduate. Ceremonies are meaningful and help us ready ourselves for the next phase or change in our lives.

A dress rehearsal is a type of ceremony. In theatre, just before opening or "going live," actors put on full costume and make-up and rehearse as if they are in front of a paying audience. This allows time to adjust to costumes, make-up, and props without the pressure of doing so in front of an audience.

Project dress rehearsals serve the same purpose: a chance to adjust and find problems without impacting the live system. The project team, go-live support team, and business walk through the script of go-live. Sometimes the training environment is used to help simulate using the system for common office scenarios.

As an undergraduate, I majored in theatre and was involved in many productions. After graduation, I worked as a professional actress before pursuing my master's degree in communication and training & development. In theatre, there is a specific step-by-step approach to rehearsing a show.

Step 1: Read through – All cast members attend and read the entire script aloud. This ensures everyone knows the story of the play and hears all of the characters in the play interacting.

Step 2: Blocking – The script is divided into scenes or sections. The director guides the actors on where to move during each section, as movement helps convey the story of the play and meet the director's vision.

Step 3: Rehearse – Actors begin rehearsing small segments of the play with script in hand and blocking. An important part of memorization is physical movement, so rehearsing helps memorization of lines and movement. Rehearsal is held daily. Eventually actors must rehearse "off book," meaning they no longer have the script in hand to assist them as they rehearse the scenes.

Step 4: Run-through – Performing multiple scenes together. For example, a run-through of Act One would be a start-to-finish performance of Act One. Eventually, cast and crew run through the entire play.

Step 5: Dress Rehearsal – Performance of the entire play with costumes, make-up, props, lighting, and set. This gives actors and crew time adjust and allows the director to determines if changes should be made to express the director's vision of the play.

Step 6: Opening night (Go-live) – When an audience watches the performance. It's thrilling for actors and crew to experience the play with the audience, who laughs and responds to events as they unfold. After the show opens, there are ongoing adjustments to be made. The director works with the stage manager to provide notes to actors about changes in their performances. This is true go-live support. Continual tweaking and coaching ensures that the performance realizes the vision of the director.

Readiness = practice + performance

Rehearsal Leads to Transformation

When I was young, my father would take our family to high school football games on Friday nights. I loved the energy and excitement of the games: the cold air and bright lights, the cheering and marching band, but the highlight for me was the cheerleaders. I wanted to be a cheerleader more than anything. I loved the uniforms, cheers, and enthusiasm they displayed. I decided then and there my goal in life was to be a cheerleader. I practiced cartwheels and flips in my front yard for hours at a time on the summer evenings.

When I entered high school, I tried out for the freshman football cheerleading squad. I didn't make it. I tried out for the basketball cheering squad. I didn't make it. I tried out for the lowliest of all cheering squads, the Wrestlerettes. I stood by the phone all night waiting for the call. I didn't make it.

As a sophomore, I tried out for the pom-pom team. Even with years of dance classes under my belt, I didn't make it. So, I made a plan. I became friends with the cheerleaders. I went to practices and games, both home and away, and watched what they did and how they did it. I observed how they interacted and how they prepared for games. I rehearsed my "cheerleading" personality with them. I learned how to yell out a cheer in an unembarrassed, uninhibited way. I practiced by doing the cheers in the stands while watching the cheerleaders. I learned to join in with the group instead of standing outside of them and how to interact in an outgoing way, rather than with my usual shyness.

At the end of my sophomore year, I tried out for varsity cheerleading... and I made it! I was the only varsity cheerleader who had never cheered before. I was over the moon with happiness. I loved cheering at varsity football and basketball games and marching in parades.

The experience taught me a great deal about the importance of rehearsal. All the time I spent with the cheerleaders amounted to rehearsal for me. Practicing how to act and be like a cheerleader helped me to prepare and be ready when opportunity presented itself.

"Developing the support plan sounds harder than it is," said Allie. Elizabeth was relieved to hear this as she was stressed about how to prepare a support plan.

"It's easy," said Jake. "Just think of worst-case scenario," he grinned.

"I kind of figured that," sighed Elizabeth.

"Start by envisioning every place where somebody might run into a problem, and then plan for how we're going to help them. This includes the help desk, an onsite team who can travel to troubleshoot, bulletins, job aids, additional training, user access teams, and of course a command center, which will be staffed nonstop for the first five days of go-live," Allie explained.

Elizabeth looked at Jake for help saying, "How the heck do I know what we need? I mean, I'm not sure how to just create a help desk!"

Allie chimed in, "I understand. You know how I thought everything was figured out for my move? I planned and thought I was ready. But *when the movers came, things got confused, and our numbered boxes didn't get loaded on the truck in the right order. We each had a suitcase with a change of clothes, some snacks, and movies downloaded on our devices to keep the kids busy. There was just one thing I overlooked,"* Allie admitted, *"I forgot to pack the kids' birth certificates and immunization records for the new school. They were somewhere in a box marked 'Office.' So even though we had our clothes, socks and shoes, the kids couldn't go to their first day of school, because we couldn't find that essential information."*

She didn't like to admit it, but Elizabeth was somewhat relieved that Allie had missed a step in her move. It seemed like things never went wrong for Allie. She immediately felt guilty for the thought.

"Now, this is just a one-family, small move," Allie continued. "When we're looking at a large technology change, we must plan for the changes we know about and recognize there will be surprises. There's always something that we aren't aware of or that was just missed. We'll need a command center, a physical and virtual place where the project teams, technical folks, leadership, training team, and business owners can convene and monitor progress of the implementation."

Elizabeth tried to conceal the worry in her voice. "Will the business and technical teams be expected to be there all day?" She could already hear the objections from the business.

"We'll set up a schedule of mandatory calls and adjust based on how things are going." Allie was already drawing on the white board.

"The goal is to provide nearly instant support for those people who are running into issues when we go live," Jake added, looking up from his phone. "As a part of the command center, we need a way to create tickets for issues. The current help desk already uses a system which can help us identify implementation issues, such as technical problems, user error, or hardware snafus. And we need to make sure that we have the essentials, meaning we know where to get the paper records and reports so we can double check things as needed."

Allie looked embarrassed at the reference to her own move mishap.

"Is that so we can see if the data is accurate? Do we need reports printed the day before to check against?" Elizabeth asked, remembering the chaos that ensued when they had implemented the new payroll system and couldn't access paystubs.

"Yes," said Jake. "Even though we don't expect issues, it's important for us to be able to check against paper reports from the day before cut-over."

"Okay," Elizabeth said, joining Allie at the white board. "Please help me figure out the command center so we can focus on the help desk," said Elizabeth. "I can't imagine how we'll pull this off without excellent support."

Technology change requires support. Most organizations have an IT help desk, which can be trained to assist with new implementations and help users manage the change.

Provide in-depth training and a practice environment to the help desk team to make sure they are prepared to assist. During go-live, pair trainers with the help desk to cross-pollinate the information between the two groups. Trainers have in-depth knowledge of how the system works, and the help desk has in-depth knowledge of where users and stakeholders are struggling.

Each business area identifies a liaison to check in with the project team and technical teams, to ensure everything's working as expected. A week or so after go-live, lab support can begin. Lab support is provided to users in variety of ways. The intent is to give individuals one-on-one time with a trainer or coach to assist them with their work and to resolve issues with them in the live system (also called *production*).

Measurement is an important aspect of support. The purpose of a measurement plan is twofold: (1) to understand how prepared end users and other stakeholders feel at various milestones in the change journey, and (2) to determine whether our activities are having the intended result. Use a survey tool and subject matter experts to develop questions for stakeholders. This will help you understand how prepared people feel about new processes or the new system. Surveys and interviews work well to identify how productive people feel, or how productive they really are, after change is implemented.

Surveys work well to measure the effectiveness of communication and identify barriers or roadblocks to adoption. Surveys don't need to be long. Sometimes just a couple of questions will identify if you are meeting your success criteria and can provide narrative responses for leadership.

Focus groups can provide detailed understanding around process. Use them to discuss specific questions about the change effort. Focus groups benefit from skilled facilitation. If run well, they may also be helpful in developing ideas and suggestions to encourage adoption.

Interviews and observation through practice labs, training, one-on-one work sessions, and meetings offer opportunities to observe actual practices and challenges for a variety of stakeholders. Observation is an in-depth form of measurement that is often overlooked in the "heat" of go-live. Outlining specific tasks and processes to observe, and using a formal tracking tool, can provide a deeper level of information and evaluation that is often difficult to obtain.

Dress Rehearsal for the Physician Practice Electronic Medical Record System

As the change lead for a regional health care system implementing an Electronic Medical Records, I was responsible for preparing physicians and their office staff to use the new system in the course of their work. This system was being implemented in more than two dozen physician practices in an eighteen-month period. We scheduled a dress rehearsal for each office. The day before system go-live, each office would close at noon, and dress rehearsal would begin.

Using the quality assurance (QA, or test) version of the system, members of the project team would act as "patients." Each patient had a scenario, medical record, and persona prepared in the QA system. Records had been created with health history, drug allergies, and problem lists to give the office staff and physicians a realistic experience of conducting a visit with the patient using the EMR system. The goal was to provide the office with the experience of using the EMR system to register, assess, treat, and bill patients in a safe environment.

After all the visits were completed, everyone involved would meet to debrief the experience. Process gaps and handoff problems were discovered. Printing seemed to always be an issue. We discussed how to flag when a patient who was ready to be seen by the physician. The dress rehearsal provided a realistic patient and process flow. It also provided a sense of relief to the staff who felt more prepared to go live after the rehearsal.

READY-Set-Change Reflections

1. Did you find problems with handoffs between the staff and the system in the rehearsal?

2. Were you able to complete your tasks using the system? If not, has it been determined why not?

3. How will you recover if you are unable to use the system for some reason? What is your back-up plan?

4. Was the team able to resolve issues after the rehearsal and document the resolution plans?

READY, Set, Change!

010

Sustaining and Maintaining the Future State

....

"Sorry I'm late," Elizabeth panted.

"No problem," said Allie. She proceeded cautiously, "Is everything okay? You seem to be running behind all the time lately."

Elizabeth could see Allie's concern and sighed. "I'm getting divorced," she admitted. "My husband just moved out, and I'm having a hard time getting everyone to school on time."

"Oh, I'm so sorry!" Allie gasped.

"I really don't want to talk about it, though," said Elizabeth.

"I understand." After an awkward pause, Allie changed the subject. *"Well, let's focus on sustaining the change then. Sustainability is something to plan for before going live. We need to consider who will be responsible for the processes, ongoing training and support, and how this transition will occur."*

"Why do we have to do this before go-live? We already have so much to do!" Elizabeth felt like she might cry out of frustration.

"I know," Allie reassured her. *"The reason we make our plans before go-live is because we know it's easier to negotiate now. Once we go live, it'll be hard to find time and clear vision with the business about who will take over the operational tasks of maintaining the new system. I'll give you an example. You told me a new Learning Management System was recently implemented. Which department or area is responsible for it?"* Allie paused to let Elizabeth answer.

"Well," Elizabeth considered, *"HR is considered the 'business owner' because we 'own' employee records. But the Training and Development Center of Excellence actually loads the training in the system and tracks CEUs and course completion. I think Nursing manages their own courses, too, but that's new."*

"Great. Now, was that all worked out before the system went live?" Allie prodded.

"No, we had a bit of a fight about it. Training and Development thought they should be the only area able to load and edit information

in the system. It took about a year to work out who could do what and when, and it's still evolving," said Elizabeth.

"Well, imagine if you'd had those discussions before go-live. You would have had an easier time figuring out who could do what to get the most out of the system. Assigning timelines for when business owners must become responsible for systems can help in hiring decisions and developing the team as well. In the post-go-live support period, we're in response mode. That phase won't last forever, though, and knowing who will be responsible for the operational support of the system can help us sustain the change in a predictable and steady way."

"Well, that makes sense," Elizabeth admitted. "I really like this idea and can see how planning before go-live helps us in the long run. I think I could use this in my personal life, too. I need a plan. Maybe I can enroll the kids in before-school care. Then I wouldn't be so stressed out each morning. Not to mention late."

Sustainability sometimes feels like the "bridge too far" after preparing for and consistently moving toward change. It takes a lot of effort to make it to go-live and through post-launch support. It seems you should be able to relax and bask in the glow of a change well done. But you must continue to strive toward sustainability. To sustain something means to strengthen or support physically or mentally. It also means to undergo or suffer. Both meanings can be applied to how stakeholders feel after a change. Sustainability refers to the ability maintain performance at a certain rate or level. Planning for sustainability is also a part of the "why."

It may feel like a puzzle to sustain change. Once you've decided how you'll measure progress toward adoption, be diligent in monitoring your metrics and adjusting your approach. Change is adopted at different speeds by individuals, who all have unique perspectives and experiences. Some people naturally need more time to become comfortable with the new world. Closely monitor the number of new demands on everyone's time to allow for different learning curves.

One of my clients called me in despair. They were struggling with the sustainment phase of their large reorganization and business structure change. As I listened to the leader, I could hear they were pursuing many initiatives at once, with the hope of shoring up the flagging morale and general confusion around the change. They had contracted with a large, well-known training organization to train on trust. They also set a large and visible goal to process map nearly 2,000 processes for redesign. A separate leadership program was underway from another training company, and executives were struggling with sending coherent communication out to the teams. What became clear was they didn't have a "through line" or a unifying story. They weren't clear on what they were doing and why this change mattered, which was creating difficulty in sustaining and gaining benefit from the change.

Without a clear, compelling story to keep the team focused on "why" a change matters, it's difficult to sustain the level of effort required for real transformation. The support and events meant to help sustain can't overwhelm or distract people from the change you are implementing. Finally, leaders must have a clear understanding of how sustainment activities support the overarching change. The challenge is to create activities which engage, but that are not so ambitious that they distract from adoption of change.

READY-Set-Change Reflections

1. Will there be major changes in who will have operational responsibility after implementation?

2. Do you expect any disagreement or "territory" issues around which business group will want operational responsibility?

3. What does your Sponsor believe should happen in terms of sustainability?

4. What types of activities may support engagement and adoption?

READY, Set, Change!

011

Crossing the Finish Line

"Oh my gosh!" thought Elizabeth. "How did I get myself into this?"
Elizabeth was lining up for the Harborside half marathon and was
nervous – no, not nervous – terrified!

Jake was somewhere up in front with the faster runners. He'd given
her a thumbs-up sign before he disappeared into the crowd.

Elizabeth took a deep breath and reviewed her checklist in her mind:
favorite shoes, comfy shorts, mindset for the tough times. She had
trained and prepared. She'd overcome her own resistance to running
and now looked forward to it each day. Because of her training and
preparation, she believed in herself and felt truly ready.

"So, this is the difference," she thought. "I am ready! I'm ready because of my preparation and mindset. And now I know how to help others become ready, too." A whistle shrieked and jolted her out of her thoughts. She laughed at herself, "Thinking about being ready has made me not ready."

She heard the announcer say, "Ready! Set!" and then the starting horn blared. Everyone started moving at once, and for a moment she began to panic. But her feet kept moving, and she felt her body adjusting to her normal pace. She began to feel like herself as the group thinned. Elizabeth was content to keep a steady pace with the two women next to her and quickly got lost in her thoughts.

She worked to remember what Jake had said about maintaining her pace and looked around for mile markers along the route. Surprised to see the six-mile mark already, Elizabeth realized that she had been aiming too low by thinking of running the 10K.

"I'd be disappointed if I was already almost done," she realized. She kept running and breathing, trying not to look at the time or markers. As she passed the nine-mile marker, her calves started to ache, and she felt like her stride was off. Her brain began to work against her, telling her that she should just stop because she had proven herself enough. Elizabeth tried to shake off the negative voice in her head by thinking about the river she'd pass at mile eleven.

Now that she thought of it, Jake was pretty smart. He'd warned her that she might begin feeling negative and that she should pick something to look forward to seeing near the end of the race.

"I always look forward to pancakes after the run," Jake confided.

Elizabeth thought about the value of knowing there would be difficulty ahead and having a plan for how to combat it. She began to think about her go-live support plan when she realized she was heading over the river. She was almost done! Now there were more people lining the route. She grabbed a cup of Gatorade from an extended hand and focused on the cheers, signs, flags, and her growing excitement as she kept putting one foot in front of the other.

"I can do it! I can do it!" she silently chanted. As she neared the finish, she gave an extra push of speed, just to feel she could. She had done it! She'd finished a half marathon!

The combination of relief and exhilaration was overwhelming, and for a moment Elizabeth was afraid she might cry. She headed to the water station, where Allie gave her a high five. "Brilliant! Congratulations!"

"Let's see if we can watch Jake cross the finish line," Allie said.

As they made their way through the crowd, Elizabeth was amazed that Jake was running twice as far as she had. She was feeling shaky. And now that she knew what it took to keep going, she was even more impressed that he was running the full marathon.

She and Allie grabbed a spot to cheer on the runners near the finish line. Allie had found a foil blanket for Elizabeth, who was starting to shiver. They looked at the pace clock and figured Jake would be there soon.

Elizabeth spotted him. "Go, Jake! Great job!" she shouted.

Allie was jumping up and down next to her, screaming Jake's name as he crossed the finish line.

"Wow," Elizabeth said. "We both finished. We did it!"

"Of course you did!" said Allie. "You got yourselves ready! You both trained with and advocated for each other, even when you felt too busy.

"You developed a support team with work friends and your families. Most importantly, you kept your 'why' in front of you, especially when you could feel you were becoming resistant. That's a winning combination!"

Elizabeth felt a bit embarrassed by Allie's assessment, but realized that is was true.

Suddenly Jake appeared, covered in sweat and holding a Gatorade in each hand. "Woohoo, we did it!" He gulped his drinks, high fived Allie, and gave Elizabeth a sweaty side hug. "I'm proud of us! Great job!" he yelled.

A dark-haired guy in jeans appeared from the crowd and gave Jake a bear hug, not seeming to notice the sweat. "This is Keith," Jake said. "Keith, this is Allie, the change guru. And you know Elizabeth, my training partner and general partner in crime."

"Congratulations!" Keith hugged Elizbeth even though she was still drenched in sweat.

"I've heard a lot about you," Keith smiled to Allie. "Wow, what an accomplishment. I'm pretty sure this is deserving of a huge stack of pancakes. Let's meet at the Log Jam and replace all of the carbs you burned off. I'm buying."

"Finally," Jake mock whispered to Elizabeth.

After more pancakes than she'd ever eaten, Elizabeth was ready to go pick up her boys from their dad's apartment. "You'll probably feel good today, but after that you'll feel like you've been hit by a truck," Jake leaned over to tell her.

"What!" Elizabeth glared at Jake. "Why didn't you tell me that before?" She was already feeling a little stiff.

"Would you have done it if you had known how hard it was?" Jake asked.

"Probably not," shrugged Elizabeth.

"Are you happy you did it?" Jake prodded.

"Absolutely," she grinned. "I feel like I finally completed a goal!"

"That's because you were ready. Hope to see you at work tomorrow," Jake added as he jumped into Keith's Jeep and waved goodbye.

Elizabeth waved goodbye and thought about what she had accomplished. She now knew how it felt to thoroughly prepare, both physically and mentally, and to plan for problems and distractions along the way. She understood that flexibility and agility was not a weakness but a strength. She had fought through her own resistance. She finally considered herself ready to lead change.

Depending on the project, go-live can either be surprisingly anti-climactic or a whirlwind of activity. As people begin to use the system, the project and technical teams are on standby to resolve unanticipated issues or see if things will work as expected. When a go-live is anti-climactic, the team is relieved But after so much preparation, it might be a bit of a let-down. Some of the toughest implementations I've worked on were anti-climactic at first, but after a day or so issues were discovered, then compounded by the continued use of the system. If a go-live starts with problems immediately, it can create a sense of emergency which can sometimes be hard to break, even after things eventually calm down.

The command center is usually set up in a conference or training room. Projecting the issue and problem tickets, which are logged by the project team, help desk, or technical team, enables the team to review and prioritize together. Depending on the size of the implementation, the command center it may be divided into zones or functionality groupings. It's ideal to have a separate room for troubleshooting. This keeps the noise level down in the command center. Food is essential, but again should be in a separate area to reduce distractions. A stand-up meeting for all assigned stakeholders should be held at least three times a day for the first three days of go-live. To start, us a cadence of 8 am, Noon, and 5 pm. Depending on the type of work, such as for 24-hour shifts, meetings may need to be held every four hours, around the clock. It is much more difficult to convene a meeting than to cancel one, so schedule the meetings as the default, and cancel if all is well and there's nothing to discuss.

READY, Set, Change!

012

Celebration!

"Can you flip those pancakes a bit faster?" Jake was in front of Elizabeth with an empty plate. "I'll take at least ten," he joked.

"Hey thanks for coming!" Elizabeth smiled, "we couldn't have done it without you."

Jake tried to wave off her thanks, but she could tell he was pleased.

'Destination DMS' had been live for three weeks. Elizabeth was proud of the messaging.

They'd used the idea that DMS was the airport code for the preflight to the EMR. She loved the posters that said, "Our 13 tons of paper won't fit in our suitcase or meet the flight weight requirement!" and

"We can't begin our EMR journey if we don't pack for our trip! We need the assistance of each physician and their staff to pack!" Packing meant scan charts and documents, uploading them, and checking that charts were correctly filed.

The project leaders were hosting a pancake breakfast for those involved with the success of the project.

Elizabeth preferred making pancakes to frying bacon. *"Have you seen Allie? I wanted to give her a big stack, too. There's no way we could've made this happen without her help."*

"Is she asleep in the command center?" Jake quipped, *"Maybe she's granting an angel it's wings."*

Elizabeth rolled her eyes at him. Elizabeth had created pins that looked like pilot wings. The physicians received their wings when everyone on their team, such as assistants and staff, attended training and process sessions and "packed" the materials assigned to them.

The wings had become so popular with the doctors that neither Allie or Elizabeth could go anywhere in the hospital without a crowd following them and requesting wings.

"The only wings I'm interested in are buffalo wings," Allie announced as she appeared in front of Elizabeth with a plate full of bacon. *"And pancakes please."*

"Of course," Elizabeth said and slid a stack on to Allie's plate. *"Allie, I really want to thank you,"* Elizabeth said. *"We couldn't have done this*

without you. You've been such a support and have given me the tools to lead change in any situation. You're amazing!"

"It was my pleasure, and you're welcome," Allie replied.

"I hope it's not time for hugs," Jake muttered.

"Don't worry Jake, you're safe. But I do have a personal matter to discuss with Elizabeth, if you don't mind." Allie said.

"I know when I'm not wanted, for hugs or gossip!" Jake headed off to the coffee line. Elizabeth was nervous, she wondered if Allie had bad news about something she'd done.

"This may or may not be helpful, but I wanted to let you know that since I've moved, we have a new childcare provider. My previous provider lives close to you and is looking for a new family to care for. She's like a second mother to my kids, in fact they may like her better than me!" Allie smiled and handed Elizabeth a card. "I thought you might want to call her. You really did a fantastic job on this project Elizabeth. Congratulations!"

Allie gave her a wave and disappeared into the crowd.

Elizabeth looked at the card and, for the first time in a while, felt a surge of hope.

Celebrations help people relax, refresh, and reflect after the hard work of implementation. There's no right or wrong way to celebrate, although food is almost always involved. Recognition and reward are important to teams. After working hard for many weeks to implement new systems or programs, it's a welcome break. For large, multi-year projects, people need to celebrate milestones and victories along the way.

One of my favorite celebrations was years ago with a team that did a fantastic job reorganizing their Purchasing department. Prior to the change the entire Accounts Receivable staff all performed essentially the same job, and everyone was a generalist. The reorganization created a three-tiered structure. Tier 1 was the customer interface. All phone calls and emails started in Tier 1 were routed to other tiers based on need. Tier 1 had a target of reaching 90 percent resolution for customers so they wouldn't need to be transferred to other areas. Within the first six months of operation, they had reached a 95 percent resolution rate, surpassing their goal.

Tier 2 processed invoices and, without interruptions from customers, they improved their processing time by 65 percent. Tier 3 was for specialized troubleshooting, focused on solving the more complex issues that previously had caused the workflow to come to a halt. Everyone on the team had done a great job staying positive through a physical move, as well as new work assignments, and were working well together in new teams.

To celebrate, we had an Academy Awards party. We rolled out a remnant of real red carpet, and the team came dressed up and posed for our "paparazzi" with feather boas, sunglasses, tiaras, and top hats we provided. Each team won a "best something" award and gathered to hold their Oscar statue and give shout outs and thanks to each other for the roles they played in making the implementation a success. The sight of the Purchasing staff strutting on the red carpet in their sunglasses, boas, and pocket protectors to accept their awards was priceless. But watching them enjoy lunch with their colleagues and share pride in their accomplishments is one of the highlights of my career.

The READY-Set-Change Model is a faster, more efficient, and less intimidating approach to change than what is used by many organizations. What's more, the READY-Set-Change Model and tools are flexible and adaptable to fit the timeline and resources of most projects. Start by putting yourself in the shoes of those who will be experiencing the change. Adopt their perspective to determine how to help them prepare physically, mentally and with clear support. You'll see higher rates of adoption, greater work satisfaction, and easier, faster implementations which lead to successful change.

Final Thoughts

Over the past twenty years, it's become clear to me that providing organizational change management has made a positive difference for people who are in the midst of change.

One of the difficulties is knowing where you are in the implementation and what to do to help. Of course, there are many factors that impact our readiness for change. My goal of including a narrative in this book was to show how concepts are put into action and to recognize that readiness can apply to personal events as well as impact our professional lives.

The READY-Set-Change Model can help by providing a framework to follow.

The tools and resources mentioned throughout the book can be found at

ReadySetChangeBook.com

You'll find the following resources there:

◊   RSC Impact Assessment
◊   RSC Stakeholder Identification and Assessment
◊   RSC Sponsor Plan
◊   RSC Communication Plan

◇ RSC Measurement Plan
◇ RSC Transition to Sustainability Plan

In my hope to provide guidance on leading change, I also want to introduce an organization which has guided me in my growth as a change leader. The Association for Change Management Professionals (ACMP) is the leading education and professional networking organization for change thought leaders and practitioners around the world.

Visit ACMPGlobal.org to download a free copy of *The Standard for Change Management*. As a Certified Change Management Professional™, I'm proud to have been one of the authors of *The Standard*.

I highly recommend connecting with ACMP, the Project Management Institute (PMI.org), or the Society of Human Resource Management (SHRM.org) to ensure you are ready to lead change.

Acknowledgements

I want to acknowledge and thank my wonderful husband, Jay, and our children, Kegan (Alyssa), Violet, Emma, Drew, Melanie, and Lily.

I also want to thank my friends who read the manuscript at different stages and offered their insights, wisdom, enthusiasm and suggestions: Cathy Fyock, Lori Kleiman, Amy Allen, Laurie Brown, Susan Cook, Joanne Cumiskey, and Gina Carr.

Thank you also to Amy Waninger for her enthusiasm and dedication, and to the many colleagues and friends who've helped me form the ideas at the heart of READY, Set, Change.

Made in the USA
Middletown, DE
28 March 2020

87327156R00096